MW00366726

Problem Child

The View
From
The Principal's
Office

IMPROBABLE TALES
FROM A
HYPERACTIVE CHILDHOOD

by

Robb Lightfoot

Copyright © 2015 Robb Lightfoot
Published by

Thinking Funny ™
www.ThinkingFunny.com
PO Box 5286
Chico, CA 95928
530-636-0550

All rights reserved.

Print
ISBN-13: 978-0-9887854-6-5
eBook
ISBN-13: 978-0-9887854-7-2
Audiobook
ISBN-13: 978-1-940986-99-9

DEDICATION

In loving memory of Mr. Tom Lewis, Principal of Highland Elementary school, who spent many a long hour trying to sort me out. Thank you for your infinite patience, Mister Lewis. You were firm, kind, and not paid nearly enough to deal with the likes of me.

CONTENTS

PREFACE

This book is dedicated to my principal, but really it's a tribute to all the teachers and parents who draw the short straw and get a kid like me. As these stories reveal, I'm loud and restless, and I have trouble following "simple instructions."

It's not that I try to be bad—usually—it's just that the unwritten rules of normal, proper, and socially-acceptable behavior don't come easily to me. Math, science and the inner workings of gadgets are a cinch to understand. But etiquette? Forget it. I mean, why will people say they're "glad to see you," and then run off before you get a chance to spend a brief three or four hours talking about the fascinating similarities between the Space Shuttle and the Millennium Falcon?

I guess I'll have to ask Karin, my wife of more than 30 years. She and her elbow alert me when it's time to quit talking technology and ask people about their jobs, kids, or dogs. It's mostly because of her that I'm now considered a member of civilized society.

But it's an ongoing, endless, and repetitive battle. It's much like the task facing those poor souls who paint the Golden Gate Bridge. Just when the job seems almost done… they have to start all over again.

I guess being ADHD is something one never really outgrows.

***

I am asked if these stories are true, and I tell my friends that they are not a memoir but rather a sorta-was.

Many of these stories happened more-or-less as written, but no doubt others would offer a different account. Some are outright whoppers that I told to amuse or redirect my parents' attention. This was often the best way to avoid other stories of shenanigans that I didn't want to share. Others here are a blend of several incidents, or a "take off" on something that happened but has, as my family will tell you, grown to mythic proportions in the retelling.

In almost every case, I was the architect of my own misfortune, and I received pretty fair treatment at the hands of my parents, school authorities, and friends.

In most cases I've changed the names of my classmates to protect their secrets. In one or two cases I've retained the actual names. I did this when I thought the stories saluted their intelligence or loyalty.

So, if you are reading this, were in my class, and come off well... then I was writing about you. But if you think the kids described here were stinkers, then, clearly, I'm talking about somebody else.

For everyone else, if you want to know which stories are "real," then email me. All of them attempt to capture the spirit of what it's like to be that kid who just can't keep still or pipe down.

The happy ending to all these tales is that most of us active kids grow up and find our place in the world. We just need some kindness, a little help, and a bit of patience.

OK. So we need a lot of patience.

But we're worth it ... aren't we?.

one

TRUTH OR CONSEQUENCES

During the first three days of Mrs. Reyes' class, I spent more time in the principal's office than most kids do during their entire grade school education.

You see, I had a fundamental misunderstanding of what teachers wanted. When they asked a question, I thought they *really* wanted an answer. Mrs. Reyes would write something on the board, saying each word as she wrote it, and I'd shout out an answer before she'd gotten halfway through the question. That's the way I'd seen it done on TV Quiz shows like *What's My Line* and *Keep Talking*.

I thought that the 1st grade would be just like that. The first one with the right answer wins. That approach, though, just gets you a hall pass to the office with the big green door.

I was shipped off to see Mr. Lewis, our principal—the "P-A-L type of principal"—Mrs. Reyes told me, "because he's your pal." He smiled as he read the note from Mrs. Reyes, and then he softly and patiently explained to me how a first grader should go about answering a question that was being written ever so slowly on the chalkboard. The method was simple: I was to raise my hand and be called upon.

"Do you understand?" Mr. Lewis asked.

"Yes sir," I answered, newly enlightened. Mr. Lewis called the matter "just a simple misunderstanding." He patted my on the head, wrote a note, and promptly returned me to the classroom.

The rest of the day proceeded uneventfully, no problems, except that Mrs. Reyes seemed to have trouble with her eyes. She didn't call on me. Not once, even though I put my hand up each time she asked a question.

I thought about this all that day and part of the night. So, when the next day dawned, I had a plan. Whenever she asked a question, I thrashed my arm to and fro, right arm supported at the elbow by my left hand, the way a drill team might wave our nation's flag, and gasped "Ooh! Ooh! I know! I know! I knooow!"

This bought me my second trip to the principal's office. It didn't take nearly as long on day two for me to be ushered in to see Mr. L. I thought that was a hopeful sign. We were beginning to work on a deeper, more personal relationship! Mr. Lewis did have less to say this time, and he got right to his point.

He sighed, rubbed his nose, and then said simply: "All you need to do, son, is raise your hand and wait your turn."

OK, I thought, this is beginning to make sense. It's all about academic minimalism—sort of a conservation-of-energy approach to education.

I smiled at this nugget, nodded vigorously, and back to the classroom I went ... to wait.

Waiting, as it turns out, was the real lesson in Room 2. Mrs. Reyes would squeak the chalk across the board, saying her sing-song words. The second I got the drift of the question, I'd shoot my hand up, straining for altitude, but more-or-less still, and I waited. I waited, and I waited, and I waited some more.

What I was waiting for was something of a mystery to

me. Mrs. Reyes would ask a question. But no one else seemed have an answer, or at least no one wanted to raise their hands, so it was pretty clear that Mrs. Reyes *ought* to be calling on me a *lot* sooner. She'd call on people who weren't even raising their hands. Again, I spent all my free time puzzling this out. It was like I was invisible. Maybe her glasses needed fixing. I knew that Mr. Lewis didn't want me to wave my arms or talk out of turn. The next morning, I again awoke with the perfect solution. I decided that I just needed a bit more visibility. So, when she asked her first question, I held my hand up high.

And I stood on my chair.

This was day three and trip number three to the principal's office. This time, he was a lot less my PAL and a lot more PO'd, a term I'd learned from my father. Dad, as it turns out, knew his principal pretty well, too.

I wasn't invited to sit down this time. Mr. Lewis began talking before the door was closed.

"Robb," Mr. Lewis began, "I think we need to meet with your parents about your classroom behavior." He looked at me over the top of his wire-rimmed glasses, and waited for an explanation. But I just stared at him. I didn't know then, but standing in your chair, even when you've got a *super-perfect* answer, is not considered appropriate behavior. So, I got to spend my Wednesday after school play time waiting in the principal's office until my mother could come over and have a little chat.

Mr. Lewis believed in the power of repetition, because the speech he gave my mother was, word for word, the same speech he'd given earlier. Then he turned to me and asked if I understood the problem. I told him that I sure did, because he'd said *exactly* the same thing, word for word, twice now, except that he said it a lot nicer the second time, when my mom was in the room. There was a silence after I made this observation, and Mom broke it.

"Thank you, Mr. Lewis, I'm sure we won't have any more problems with Robb answering questions."

Mr. Lewis smiled at her and frowned at me. The amazing thing was he could do both of these things at the same time. I wouldn't have believed it possible if I'd not seen it happen, right there. Maybe it was a requirement of being a principal, a biological oddity like my chameleon Godzilla, who could move his eyes independently of one another.

When we returned home, Mom told me that I needed to quit answering questions, at least for a while.

"But Mom. How can I? Mrs. Reyes asked if anyone knew, and I *know!*"

"Yes, I know that you know. So does Mrs. Reyes. That's why she doesn't call on you. She wants your classmates to talk. I want you to help her out. Don't say anything when she wants others to have a turn."

"But how will she know I know?"

"Teachers can tell," Mom said.

"But… how?"

"They *know,*" Mom said with a note of finality. She tilted her head forward and fixed her eyes on me. This was her "enough is enough look," meaning it was the end of our discussion and it had better be the end of the problem. I didn't argue, but part of me still suspected that Mrs. Reyes was just getting old.

I did manage to end the week without going to the principal's office again because of my mother's sage advice. The next week was going well, until Wednesday.

That morning, we had a substitute, Mr. Golden, and he called roll. One by one, he asked if each of us was present.

Then he got to my name, asked the same question for the 12th time, and looked around the room.

I hesitated and pondered my next move. There were at least two reasons to *not* answer.

First, as Mom said, he was giving everyone else a chance to talk. So I should keep quiet.

Second, since all the seats were full, he could tell we were all here, it was a question he *knew* that I could answer.

I smiled and held my tongue. *Mom will be so pleased.*

Then Mr. Golden frowned, cleared his throat, and used his loud yard-monitor voice to ask again: *"Is Robb here?"*

Everyone swiveled their heads to look at me. But, clearly, this was a test.

And I wasn't falling for it.

After all, Mr. Golden *knew* I was there. And *I* knew that he knew. And surely *he* knew that I knew that he knew. So there's no way I'm going to get into trouble *this time.*

I kept quiet.

***

Week two, day three, trip number four to the principal's office.

I handed Mr. Lewis the referral form, and Mr. Golden had printed: **INSUBORDINATE BEHAVIOR WHEN ASKED A DIRECT QUESTION.**

Mr. Lewis scanned the note, sighed, and motioned for me to sit down.

"Isn't it a little early in the day to be having problems with your substitute teacher?" he said, pointing to the wall clock.

I dutifully looked at its big, round dial, just like the one in *Beat the Clock*. I puzzled over the question for a moment and decided to ask for a hint.

"Gee Mr. Lewis, I don't know," I shrugged. "Would later be better?"

This was the first—but not the last—time I saw his face turn red.

"Robb, do you have any idea how much trouble you're in? *Four* referrals in less than two weeks! We've already had your mother in here. We are all *very* concerned about you! What do you think we should do about this?"

Hmmm another puzzler, I wondered, *was this a bonus-round?*

I studied his face, and could feel that the pressure was on. This was like the *$64,000 question*. The right answer could have a big payoff, so I took a stab at it.

"Maybe we could buy Mrs. Reyes new glasses," I said, trying to be helpful. "And tell Mr. Golden if the seats are full, then no one is absent."

There was a long silence, but no bells rang, no lights flashed, and no one beckoned me into the winner's circle.

Finally, Mr. Lewis shook his head, stood up, and led me to a small desk in the outer office.

"Sit here and think about that answer," he said. Then he left me alone. I replayed the moment in my mind about a million times. And hours later, I *still* thought it was a pretty good answer. But Mr. Lewis disagreed. He wrote a note for me to take home to Mom.

That day I realized Highland Elementary's quizzes lacked cash payouts or consolation prizes. Worse yet, when you're sent to the office, expect a round of *Truth or Consequences*.

And losers spend the afternoon behind Door #3.

RUNS, WALKS, AND ERRORS

The playground was almost empty before I began my mad dash to my classroom. I rounded a corner, and there was Mrs. Reyes, arms folded.

"Stop. Go back. And walk," she ordered.

I slid to a halt in front of her. She was guarding the door to her 2nd grade classroom, and had apparently watched as I dashed from the far end of the playground, cut across the lawn, and hugged the hallway corners to arrive before the late-bell.

"What?" I asked, wondering what was wrong. I managed to be the last one off the playground and *still* arrive before the door closed. I thought I'd done a good job of maximizing my playtime.

"No running in the hallways," she said, pointing a boney finger back from where I came. "Go back and walk."

"Back?" I looked in at my classmates. They were craning their necks to see what was happening.

"*All the way back.*" She stabbed her finger for emphasis. Then she scowled, and waited.

I retraced my steps.

As I plodded up the corridor, she returned to her

classroom and closed the door behind her just as the bell rang.

I trudged past closed classroom doors in the suddenly silent hallway. It was creepy. All I could hear was the echo of my own footsteps. I reached the water fountain that marked the halfway point to the principal's office, and I hesitated.

Just how slow should I walk? I wondered. *She did say all the way… and I have to <u>walk</u>.* I sighed. *This will take for-ever.*

Then I began to think about what it was going to be like to walk back into the classroom.

All eyes will be on me.

Everyone will laugh.

And then I'll have to wait… to see if I'll be sent to my desk …or to the corner … or to the blackboard to scratch out some sentences of repentance.

Yuck.

Then comes the paperwork to document my misdeed—a moving violation. Another note home. I shuddered.

What will Mom say this time?

I stood there immersed in these thoughts, pondering the future, and wishing it were possible to magically appear at my desk with no one the wiser.

Maybe I could borrow HG Well's time machine and just skip the rest of the day.

All this rolled around in my brain as I leaned against the water fountain. So I didn't notice Mrs. Kelly scurrying my way. She was distracted, head down, thumbing through a stack of sheet music when she plowed into me. Both of us staggered to regain balance.

Mrs. Kelly let out a cat-like yowl, and looked up with alarm and annoyance. She was on her way to Glee Club, but her expression was not gleeful.

"What are you doing out here?" she asked.

"Mrs. Reyes sent me back," I said.

"Back?" she said. She looked around, getting her bearings. We were nowhere near the bathroom, the

8

cafeteria, or the principal's office—the only places a kid would be if not in class. "Humph," she said, and frowned. Then she glanced at the tiny silver watch on her wrist, shook her head, and straightened her stack of papers.

"Well, then, you'd better go back."

I nodded my compliance, but I was confused. Back, I thought, *to where?* I hesitated.

"Now," she said, waving her hand to dismiss me, and watched for a moment as I resumed my slow march away from my classroom. She turned and hurried on to her choir.

I reached the end of the hallway and stopped. Mrs. Reyes had told me to go *all the way* back. I looked across the playground to the far fence where I'd began my sprint. *If I go all the way out there,* I thought, *I'll be super late.*

But I remembered the look on her face and I figured that I'd better do <u>exactly</u> what Mrs. Reyes said. So, I walked, s-l-o-w-l-y, as though an adult were watching every step, across the lawn and out onto the playground, all the way to the far fence. I shuffled along the chain link, not quite sure just where I had started running. I'd been digging for gold flakes, just like the miners we'd seen in our history film. So I searched the area, looking for my claim.

There were a jillion little pits out there, but I guess that's what happens when everyone is bitten by the prospecting bug. And that's precisely why I'd stayed so long past the first bell—I was afraid of claim jumpers.

I crisscrossed the pockmarks, looking at one excavation after the next, trying to find the particular place I'd been standing when I started my run. I must have looked over a hundred holes, and still I couldn't be sure. I was absorbed with this problem when I felt a crushing force close on my shoulder.

It was Mr. Golden, the PE teacher.

"What in the Sam Hill are you doing here?" he asked. I looked at him, wondering what *he* was doing out here. I saw that he had a sack full of baseball gear, rubber bases, balls and mitts.

"I was looking for my hole," I said.

He looked at me with a pained expression.

"Your *what*?" he asked.

"My hole, sir."

He chewed his lip for a moment, and then decided he really didn't care to know why my hole was so important.

"Well, you'd better hustle back to class," he said, jerking his thumb in a gesture like I'd just been called out at home plate.

"I can't," I said.

"Oh, really?"

"No sir. Not yet." I took a deep breath, ready to explain Mrs. Reyes instructions, and how she expected me to *walk all the way back*, but I never got the chance.

"Well we'll just see about that," he snorted, and swung me up and over his back, carrying his duffle on one shoulder and me on the other. With each step, his bag clobbered my noggin.

I was seeing stars by the time he got to Mr. Lewis' waiting room.

Usually I had to wait to see the principal, but he was standing at the door for me when I was deposited with a thump. Mr. Lewis had been looking out the window, and seen us coming.

I stood up, and he led me into his office, the only carpeted room in the entire building. Out of habit, I started to dust myself off.

"Let's wait on that," Mr. Lewis said.

"OK." I stopped and stood awkwardly.

"So?" Mr. Lewis cocked his head. "Missed the late bell?"

"Ah, no sir."

"Really?"

"I was on my way to class, but Mrs. Reyes wanted me to go back to the fence."

Mr. Lewis' eye widened. He looked even more puzzled than usual.

"Following directions?" he asked.

"Just like she said," I answered.

Mr. Lewis sat down in his chair, put his hands on his brow, and massaged his temples. He rocked back and forth, shaking his head slowly. Then he sat up and pressed the intercom button.

"Mrs. Reyes," he said.

Several moments went by, and I heard a tinny but familiar voice.

"Yes, Mr. Lewis."

"Did you want Robb standing out by the fence during class?"

"What?"

"Did you tell Robb to go stand by the fence?"

"Of course not."

"Very well." Mr. Lewis looked at me warily. "He's in my office now. I'll be sending him along directly." He flipped off the intercom, and turned to face me.

"But she *did!*" I countered, before he could say a thing.

"I'm sure that's what you *heard*," he said softly. "But that's not what she *intended.*"

"Oh," I replied, absently dusting my pants off.

His phone rang, then Mrs. Earl buzzed. Mr. Lewis picked up the phone and put the hand over the mouthpiece.

"Come back at recess," he said, "and we'll talk."

I shrugged. "OK."

"Now run along to class."

I froze. "Really?"

He sighed. "What now?"

"Well Mister Lewis, that's sorta how all this started."

three

PAST AND PRESIDENT

Carl waved a sheet of binder paper in front of me.

"Can you help me with my homework?"

He knew I loved to read, talk, and share my wisdom, and I was only too glad to help.

I took the paper and tried to read his messy handwriting. It staggered forward across the page, weaving up and down, barely contained between the lines. It was even worse than mine. At the top of the page it said "Abe #16." Other than that, every second or third word was impossible to read.

"What's this?" I tried to hand the paper back to him, but Carl refused.

"Please. It's due after lunch," Carl said.

"Your writing stinks."

"Yeah. I know." He shrugged. "If I don't know how to spell a word, I just scrunch it up."

"Well," I studied the paper again. "This is pretty scrunchy."

"Let me read it to you…" Carl said.

"Abraham Lincoln was the 16th president of the United States of America. He was born when he was very young and lived between 1939 and 1962…."

Carl looked up, trying to gauge my reaction.

"Is that from an encyclopedia?" I asked.

"We don't have an encyclopedia."

"Then?"

"I looked in my dad's pants."

I wasn't sure what to make of this.

"Well," Carl said, "Abraham Lincoln is on pennies, you know."

"So?"

"I just wrote down the dates I saw."

"But every penny has a different date?"

"Stupid," Carl rolled his eyes. "Of course they do, but when you're president, they print money each year, right?"

"Yeah," I said. It was hard to argue with that.

"So, I just wrote down the first date and the last date I found. Should be about right." Carl bent back down to read some more.

"Abraham Lincoln was born on February 12th, President Lincoln's birthday, which is why everybody knew he was special and became president."

Carl looked up again. "I added that last part."

"I don't think it works that way," I said.

"Well, how do you explain that he was born on a President's birthday?"

The thing about talking to Carl was that he had a way of making this stuff sound sort of logical. He folded the paper down a bit to read on.

"President Lincoln had a Gettysburg address and lived in the White House right while he was chopping logs and fighting the Civil War. It ended, and he quit being president."

"Didn't he get shot?" I asked.

"Was that him, or the other guy?" Carl frowned.

"What 'other guy,'" I asked.

"You know. The one they shot for chopping down the cherry tree?"

13

The bell rang, signaling the end of lunch recess, and I decided that there was no real payoff to being Carl's fact checker.

"Maybe you're right." I said.

"Yeah, I think so." Carl folded his paper up. "So, which President did you get?"

"Jefferson," I said

"Which one was that?"

"Oh, you know, the guy on the $2 bill," I said. "Ever hear of him?"

"No. But my dad doesn't carry much cash."

four

SICK MICKEY

I got my first wristwatch—a genuine stem-winding Mickey Mouse timepiece—when I graduated from kindergarten.

Alas, Mickey and I didn't make it to the first grade.

The watch ran OK at first. Mom read the instructions to me and told me to wind it once a day, or "as needed." It was the "as needed" part that got me and Mickey in trouble. I checked Mickey against the Grandfather clock in the front room—"the most accurate clock in the world"— Dad claimed, and I noticed poor Mickey seemed to be a half-minute behind. So, I'd sit by the Grandfather clock until it struck one of the quarter-hours, pull out the stem, and set little Mickey aright.

But it bothered me that Mickey couldn't keep up with that old Grandfather clock, and I decided that he must need more go-power. Clearly, this was what they meant by "as needed." I took to winding Mickey every hour. It didn't take much. I tried counting the number of clicks, and two seemed about right.

But Mickey was still losing the battle with Father Time, and I thought maybe he needed three clicks, or four just to be safe. Mickey seemed to disagree, because after a few days of this treatment, he stopped altogether. I realized

15

something was wrong, and I wanted to ask my dad. He was a fixit genius, but I hated to ask him because just two days prior, we'd had "the gate incident."

***

Dad had been planning his oversized driveway-gate for ages, and finally gathered all the material and built it in single weekend. He worked morning 'till night, but he whistled and smiled the whole time he was welding and grinding.

It looked like he was having fun.

The finished product was quite a sight—10 feet long, rounded, and sleek. Dad painted it a high gloss jet black, and it pivoted elegantly on massive hinges embedded in our concrete-block walls.

Smooth bars crisscrossed in a web like pattern—just asking you to wrap your hands around them. It looked like a monkey-bar rocket ship laying on its side, waiting to be elevated into launch position. My brother Jim and I decided that all it needed was a set of fins and it could take an astronaut to the Moon.

We named Dad's gate "Jules-I."

After Dad went to work, Jim and I were all over Jules. It was a blast riding the gate through its long arc, imagining that we were on our way to lunar orbit, and then aborting our mission—jumping off—just before Jules slammed into the wall.

All our whooping and simulated rocket sounds attracted the neighborhood kids. Pretty soon they were all standing in line waiting their turn to countdown.

Jules-I was doing a brisk business on its maiden voyage.

And that was OK, except it took sooooo long to get a turn—thirty-two seconds by Mickey's reckoning—that we decided to double up. We found that two-at-a-time was faster, and three on board was even better. Jules traveled faster and faster the more people that were on him.

Clearly, our rocket ship gate enjoying being a flying, no-cost carnival ride. In a flash of inspiration, I wondered what would happen if we *all* got on the gate at once.

And for the record, I never *told* everybody to get on the gate, I just *asked* them if they'd like to try. What happened really wasn't *my* fault.

So the fateful moment came when we all piled on— there was barely room for all eight of us—and Jules shuddered a bit on liftoff. The random bobbing and weaving were a new part of the ride, and they made for exhilarating, unexpected undulations. Once, twice, three times we all jumped on the gate, and it just kept getting better … right up to the moment it exploded. We heard a "pop," a "zing," and saw a hunk of metal fly from the gate and dent Mom's station wagon.

Someone screamed: "abandon ship," and in its final act of revenge, Jules tossed us all on the concrete.

There were no media present to record the crash, and it's probably just as well. Everyone fled the scene, a few nursing scraped knees, leaving Jim and I to face Dad when he returned from work.

Just before dinner, Dad pulled up and jumped out of his truck. He walked over to where the gate should have been, but it was nowhere to be seen. We'd dragged the pieces off to the side.

So Dad stood, staring at empty space, until his eyes caught hold of the twisted remains of Jules. Jim had gone out to greet Dad, but I'd decided that caution was a better tactic.

Dad saw my kid brother, and began yelling.

"What the Hell is *this*?" he asked, stabbing his finger at the twisted tubing.

"It's a broken gate," Jim said.

"I can see that," Dad shouted.

I wondered for a moment why he'd asked, if he already knew. But I knew better than to say anything, and I kept out of sight.

"How did this happen?" Dad asked.

"We were opening it," Jim said, "and it just broke."

"I'll bet," Dad said, shaking his head. Then his eyes narrowed.

"Where's your brother?"

Jim shrugged, and then cast a nervous look over his shoulder in my direction. Dad squinted and held his hand up to shade his eyes, trying to find me.

"Robb! Get your tail over here."

I edged up to the driveway, stopping within sight but keeping a healthy distance. Dad saw me and pointed at the ground in front of him.

"Here. I want you right *here*."

I sidled up to the spot, ready to leap out of harm's way. I was relieved when I saw Mom walk out to keep a watchful eye on us.

"OK. So explain this," Dad gestured toward he demolished gate.

I looked at him, and wondered just how much to say. Should I tell him that Jules—his gate—had taken the first busload of kids to the Moon? Would he be pleased to know the entire neighborhood had spent an afternoon in utter bliss? Could he find consolation in the fact that his handiwork had *almost*, almost gotten us all the way home?

I saw Dad's red face and thought it best that the Jules-project remain in my top-secret files.

But, still, I had to say *something*.

"Everybody was really impressed with your new gate," I said. "And they were wondering how strong it was."

Dad groaned and slapped his head.

"I didn't tell them to get on the gate. Honest. They just all decided to do it."

Dad looked at me, still squinting.

"*All?* Hmmm. Were *you* on the gate?"

"At first," I admitted.

"And then?" he asked.

I wanted to tell Dad, more or less, what happened, but

it needed to be done *very carefully*. So I kept quiet, thinking hard and fast, and licked my lips.

"Well?" Dad asked.

"I think it was when Sam got on," I nodded, suddenly pleased with myself. I did some mental math, and smiled. "Yeah, that's it. Sam was just too big for the gate."

And this was one of those explanations that *almost* fit the facts, which is to say it was *mostly* true. I mean, Sam *is* two years older than me, and twice my size.

Dad looked at me and shook his head.

"Sam's a big kid, but he couldn't break the gate by himself," Dad said.

I nodded but said nothing.

"So, who else was on the gate?"

"When?" I asked.

"When it *broke*," Dad said, his face getting red again.

"A lot of kids," I said.

"And you?" Dad pressed me. "What were you doing?"

"When?" I said.

"*When the gate broke!*"

"I was on the ground," I said.

"You weren't on the gate?"

"Not after it broke,"

Dad threw his hands up and looked heavenward.

"Why *me*, God? Why?"

I knew that he'd lecture us about breaking the gate. That's what parents do, but I was a bit surprised that he was taking this so hard. After all, he'd enjoyed *building* the gate, maybe he could have fun *fixing* it too. I was thinking of pointing this out when he spoke up again.

"Son, just tell me one thing. Why'd you do it?"

I was about to say that it seemed like a good idea at the time. So often this is usually my answer to questions asked by red-faced people. And I almost told him so.

But then I realized maybe I didn't fully understand Dad's question.

I mean, I knew why *I'd* done it. But there were *eight* of

us on that gate, and maybe Dad meant "you" the same way Grandma Hitt did: "Y'all."

And why did *all* the other kids get on the fence? Hmmm, I thought, good question. Since I hadn't asked them, I couldn't say. It looked like Beverly was scared, but she wanted to be with her friend Rosey. Sam liked going fast, and my little brother Jim probably did it because he was a copycat, and did everything I did.

Who knew why they did it? I mean, when you think about it, why does anyone do anything? Were they bored? Curious? Looking for some exercise? Checking their reflexes? Dad was asking a philosophical question, one that touched on the roots of human motivation. And I had the same answer researchers the world over have when confronted with incomplete or inconclusive data: "I don't know."

My carefully considered answer didn't please Dad.

"You don't know?" Dad repeated, shaking his head.

"No sir," I said.

Dad looked up at the heavens again, probably asking God for a hall-pass to just strangle me on the spot, but since Mom was standing there, he didn't. Sensing an opening, Mom jumped in, trying to calm things down. She put her arm around Dad, gave him a hug, and whispered in his ear: "At least no one got hurt."

Dad grunted, and his shoulders slumped.

"Do you think you can fix it?" she asked.

Dad shook his head, then looked at the metal.

"Well, maybe."

"Worth a try?" she asked.

"Yeah, I guess."

"You once told me you could fix anything," Mom patted him on the back.

He laughed.

"Yeah, I did, didn't I?" Then he looked at me. "But that was before we had kids."

It was Mom's turn to laugh.

"But you're so much older and wiser," Mom said.

Dad cracked a smile.

"Definitely older," he said.

Mom gave him a peck on the cheek, and then nodded in my direction.

"Son, what do you say to your father?" This was a standard mom-question, and I had my well-rehearsed answer.

"Sorry Dad."

Dad shook his head and raised his hands in a gesture of surrender.

"You're gonna be the death of me," Dad said. Then he put his arm around Mom and shuffled away from the gate—his next home-repair project—and into the relative safety of the living room and a cold beverage.

***

Two days had gone by since the gate fiasco, and Dad had assembled all the pieces in his workshop. He heated them and hammered the bars back into their original shapes. Eventually, he was whistling a tune while he worked. I heard, and peeked in the garage. He was smiling, so I wandered up to his workbench to get a closer look.

He didn't look up.

"Nobody better come near this gate again," Dad said, "because when I'm done it'll carry a bazillion volts of electricity."

Then he looked up at me.

"And anyone who touched it will be instantly be burned to a crisp."

He then looked back down at the gate, and resumed work.

This was a good sign. Dad was telling me that the gate *was* fixable. And since he was in a good mood, and already in his workshop, I pulled my ailing Mickey Mouse out of my pocket. I wanted to ask if he could fix it, too.

"Dad," I called over the noise of the torch. Not sure if he'd heard, I repeated, "Dad."

He looked up, frowned, and snapped off the fuel. The flame let out a big "pop" and went out. Then he pulled off his mask and wiped the sweat from his face.

I dangled the watch in front of him, and he took it.

"Mickey stopped," I said.

He eyed the watch.

"Hmmm…"

"Can you fix it?"

"Hmmm…" he turned the watch over, and rubbed it between his fingers, and then touched it to his forehead just the way he'd place his brow against ours when we were feeling unwell.

I waited for him to open a tool chest, but instead he grabbed a rag and wound it around Mickey, leaving a slit that revealed only his big-little eyes.

"Good news, son. It's not broken."

I smiled, relieved for a moment."

"But he's stopped."

"Well, then there's the bad news." Dad shook his head. "Mickey's sick."

I was sad, but a bit relieved that, this time, maybe it wasn't my fault.

"What's he got?" I asked.

"Hard to say for sure." Dad stroked the watch, "But he looks pale to me. Maybe some sort of rodent fever."

"Rodent fever?"

"It happens. You know, he stands there all day, telling you the time, and he probably has skipped a few meals."

"Meals?"

"Yeah. You got to put him back in his box once and a while, so he can rest up and eat. I'll bet you've been sitting there looking at him all day."

Dad had me there.

I nodded.

"Well then maybe he just got sick on account of that,

you looking at him all day, and then him looking at you all day."

I nodded again. That *is* what I was doing.

"And he may have gotten dizzy out there riding the gate all afternoon. You didn't take him off before you got on the gate?"

I shook my head.

Dad smiled. "I thought so."

"So, what do I do?" I asked.

"Just put him back in the box and let him rest up."

"How long?" I asked.

"Well, you're getting like 12 weeks of summer vacation. Right?"

I nodded again.

"So, let him have the summer off."

"Really? Mickey needs a vacation?"

"Yep. Just give it a rest. *Everything* needs a rest now and then. Give it a try. You could sit in there, by his bedside, while he's getting better, and just talk to him."

"What?"

"Read him a magazine. Keep him out of trouble. Maybe some Reader's Digest or Boy's Life."

"OK," I said. "Thanks."

"No problem," Dad said, and then he carefully handed the cloth bundle back to me, tucking the bands into his bandage-like wrap.

I took Mickey in the palm of my hand, and patted him gently. It hadn't occurred to me that everything needs a rest. So I did as Dad said, and put Mickey back in his box. I even sat in there with him, reading him some Hardy Boys stories. It took a day or two, but eventually Mom noticed that I was spending a lot of time in my bedroom and that Mickey was missing.

"What's up?" Mom asked, "and where's your watch?"

"Dad told me that Mickey needed some sleep," I said.

Mom cocked her head and raised an eyebrow, giving me that "You've got to be kidding" look. "And *why* does

23

your watch need a nap?"

"Rodent fever." I said, proud to remember the diagnosis.

Mom shook her head, and told me to go get Mickey so she could perform her own examination. She looked him over, tapped him gently on the counter top a few times, and he woke up to run for a few minutes before nodding off. She looked at me, sighed, and shook her head.

Then we had a discussion about how you should wind a watch only once a day—no more.

She also told me that while Mickey can tell me the time of day, he *can't* tell me when it's a good time to ask Dad for help.

"So, when is the right time to ask?"

"When you're on his good side," Mom suggested.

"Oh," I said in a small voice. "But what if I'm not?"

She smiled, "I guess that could take a while. Well, just be sure I'm in the room."

"OK. But, what if you're not around?" I wondered aloud.

"Then, only ask Dad on February 31st."

"Really?" I said. "That's a real day?"

"Look it up."

She pointed towards the encyclopedias and winked. "It's right next to 'Don't Believe Everything You Hear Your Parents Say Day.'"

five

OVER THE RIVER & THROUGH THE SHOULDS

My mother tried to avoid it when she could, but at least once a month we'd pack everyone in the station wagon and go over to my grandparents' house across town. Mom dreaded these trips to her in-laws, and all of us, Dad included, were briefed on how we *should* behave and what we *should* say.

"Don't talk about our new silverware," Mom said.

"Why not?" I asked. "I thought you liked it."

Mom pursed her lips. "I do. It's just…. You don't need to bring it up, that's all."

To tell the truth, I don't think I'd have ever mentioned forks in a million years. What 10-year-old cares to discuss table settings? But now it was the forbidden flatware. It was hard to keep it out of my mind.

Dad sighed. "Anything else?"

"Now that you mention it," Mom said, "I don't want any cracks about the chicken casserole."

"What about the chicken case-of-rolls?" my little sister, Pat, asked.

"Nothing," Mom said. "Just don't talk about the chicken."

25

"Which chicken?" my brother asked.

"Any chicken, all chicken," Mom said, her voice rising. "Do I make myself clear?"

I sat in confused silence. Dad whistled a tune, and my brother Jim's GI Joe took a swing at little Pat's Barbie, who gave a deft counterpunch to Jim's arm. "Ouch."

"Keep it down back there," Dad said. "How long do you want to stay?" Dad asked Mom.

Mom gave him a sidelong stare, looking at us at the same time with the eyes in the back of her head. "Not now," she said.

"What?" Dad said, as if he'd not heard.

"Not here."

"Oh, yeah."

I had the impression that all the really interesting adult conversations, the ones that made sense anyway, happened in the big bedroom.

We arrived at my grandparents, a white stucco home that was ringed with huge sycamore trees. The biggest tree, in the back yard, had a tire swing and a decaying tree house that we were forbidden to use.

"Hi Ronnie," Grandma Toots ran out and hugged everyone but my Mom, who was holding a chocolate cake in a Tupperware container. "Oh, you shouldn't have," Grandma said to Mom, looking at the cake suspiciously. "What is it?"

"A cake," Pat said helpfully.

"I see," Grandma said.

"Chocolate and more chocolate," Jim added.

"The doctor says that your grandfather needs to cut back on the sweets. Diabetes risk," Grandma said.

Mother looked back and us, and rolled her eyes.

"Really," Dad said. "When did that happen?"

"Last month, or last year. I forget."

"Oh," Mom said. "Wish I'd known."

"Hmmm…." Grandma said, looking at Pat. "Is this a new dress?"

"Yes," Mother said quickly. "I made it last week."

"It looks a little short."

"It's a summer outfit," Mom said.

"Hmmm…" Grandma said. "And Jim is playing with dolls?"

"It's an action figure, Grandma," Jim said.

"Hmmmm….. Well, come inside everyone. Lunch has been waiting. I was expecting you half an hour ago."

"Sorry. Had some trouble," Dad said, waving his hand vaguely towards the car.

"Hmmm…." Grandma said. "You'll have to tell me over lunch."

Everyone headed towards the house, and Grandma puttered for a moment in the yard, coiling up a hose. I brought up the rear. Suddenly, she dropped the hose, and in a few quick steps she was at my side.

Grandma grabbed my hand and squeezed it, hard. "And how are you?"

"Fine, Grandma."

"You've gotten bigger," she said. "What are they feeding you?"

"Not chicken," I said carefully.

"Hmmmm…." She said. "And what else are you not supposed to talk about?"

I looked helplessly at Mother ahead of me. She was distracted with juggling the cake while opening the door. Dad had stopped to help Pat tie her shoe.

"Nothin.'"

"Hmmmm….." Grandma said, and smiled slyly. "We'll have to talk about that."

My stomach slid down to my knees, and I hadn't even been told to "eat my greens" yet. Mom saw that Grandma had me in tow, and handed the cake off to Dad. She scurried back to Grandma and me.

"He's getting so big," Grandma said. "Pity you don't feed him chicken, though."

Mother gave me an unsmiling look. "Oh, really, Toots.

Of course he eats chicken."

"Hmmm…."

"It's just not his favorite," Mom added, grasping my other hand and squeezing even harder than Grandma.

We came to the door, three abreast, unable to go through without *someone* letting go of my hand, but neither of them did right away. "Well," Grandma said. "You'll have to tell me what you're cooking these days, Martha." She let go of my hand, and Mom did an instant later.

"Yes, I really should," Mom said.

"Can I go?" I asked.

"Yes, you really should," Mom said, jabbing her finger towards the dining room.

I dashed away, my mind full of chicken and flatware.

It looked like it was going to be a long afternoon.

six

THE FINE ART OF FUSSING

I'm the big brother, and so the first kid to figure out how things work. It's not easy. I've spent hours studying my parents. As a Christmas present, I passed these tips to my kid brother and baby sister.

I think the advice helped, so I'll share them with you, too.

Begin with the fundamentals. The keys to success are timing and technique. Here are five pointers gained from years of observing parental behavior.

ASKING MOM

Step M1: Kill her with kindness. You must first put your target in the right frame of mind. For Mom, this would mean cleaning up the kitchen, sweeping or doing dishes without being asked. Extreme requests could entail mopping. We're not talking about cleaning up the mess you just made, either. This means cleaning up the mess someone else made.

Be careful here. If the room was clean the last time Mom saw it, then it doesn't count. So, you'd have to make sure she saw your little sister's effort to feed pancakes to her Barbie Dolls. You will also have to ensure that you are completely in the clear and are not implicated by a pseudo-random act of kindness.

It helps to make sure that your altruistic ploy was different than the one you used last time. Otherwise, you'll get the "And what are you up to" response.

Step M2: Be a clock watcher. Timing matters. Avoid first thing in the morning or last moment before bedtime requests. These are not taken seriously. Forget any request that comes the day before payday or within an hour of the expected arrival of any white-haired or wrinkled relative.

Step M3: Make eye contact. You've got to have her full attention. Don't try it when she's changing a diaper, on the phone, cooking, cleaning, or doing all that stuff moms seem to think is more important than listening to you. Don't try to do anything through a closed door, especially the bathroom door. It's OK to tug on her blouse if she's talking, so long as she's only talking to herself. If you hear her singing or humming a tune, drop whatever you're doing and hit her with your biggest demand.

Step M4: Put on a happy face. Good salesmanship begins with a big smile and tons of confidence. Let the enthusiasm just ooze out of your voice. Dash into the room, throw your arms open wide and announce: "Mom, I've got a great idea. Can I…." The idea may not, in fact, be all that great. And don't ask if she thinks it's a great idea. The point is that you've got to sell her on it big and fast. Don't lose heart. Remember that this is the same woman who bought a set of World Books on the installment plan, from a door-to-door encyclopedia salesman, and is still buying the yearbooks.

Step M5: Read between the lines. You need to become a student of nonverbal communication. If you have an overly complicated, multilayered, or multiple-part fuss, then you need to learn to quit while you're ahead. If the smile starts to flatten out, or you see creases at the corners of her eyes, creases that weren't there when you started your request, desist. If you see her shrug, or mumble something through a mouthful of bobby pins, assume the answer was yes. Dash out of the room and act as if you've been given the keys to the kingdom.

Try these five easy steps, and watch your success rate climb!

ASKING DAD

With Dad, you only need to concentrate on a single technique.

Step D1: Study the TV Guide, and locate the time slot for his favorite show.

Step D2: Make sure the remote is not close at hand so he can't just turn up the volume.

Step D3: Thirty seconds before show time, drag his biggest toolbox across the floor.

Step D4: Stop directly between Dad and the color TV.

Step D5: Begin with the phrase "Dad, can you help me with…." Usually, you won't even need to finish your sentence, but if he's a bit slow, drop some tools, greasy ones first.

Nine times out of ten, you'll hear: "GO ASK YOUR MOTHER!"

Then, just proceed to step M1 above.

seven

ROCK, PAPER, EXCUSES

My mother missed my kindergarten graduation. She said that she was in the hospital meeting the stork to get my little sister. But I already have a little brother, and he's not all that useful, so I don't think this is a good excuse. I asked Mom if the stork would take rejects on return trips. She smiled her big, loving smile, patted me on the head, and said, "No. And that's a good thing."

I am something of an expert in excuses, or so I have been told, because I've spent many hours using them, or as my teachers often say, "making them up."

Mrs. Reyes, my first-grade teacher, said my behavior was "inexcusable." It all began with the rock-throwing club I started during recess, a perfectly good idea that was nearly killed off by a second-grader named Susan-May Shuffleberger.

We started the club after the third-graders chased us off the swings, and the second-graders told us that *they* owned the monkey bars. This left only the sand box, and that was for the baby-kindergartners. We first-graders needed *something*, so a bunch of us first-grade boys wandered out to the far reaches of the playground to consider our options. There was no play-equipment there, so the bigger kids left us alone—at first.

The only thing out by the chain-link fence was trash that had blown in off the street—bottle caps and cigarette butts, and rocks of all sizes and shapes. This, I later learned from our principal, was excess gravel from our new sidewalks that would soon surround the school.

Since there wasn't much else to do, we kicked them around, until I kicked a particularly large rock, and noticed two things simultaneously: it sparkled as it slid through the dust, and it hurt my big toe.

Chris noticed the sparkling too, and managed to grab the crystal-rock before I could hobble over to it. A friendly disagreement ensued, where we both took turns bashing one another with this rock—proving it to be both a thing of beauty and a practical tool. We stopped our scuffling when Mike grabbed the crystal-rock, and we both took out after him. Mike was one of our class' top runners, on a good day, but when he ran to the playground's corner, Chris and I trapped him. He didn't want to participate in our small land dispute, but he didn't want to give it up, either.

So, he lobbed the rock to his friend Randy.

Of course, if you're going to throw a rock at a friend, it is a good idea to let your friend know *before* you throw the rock. Mike did call out Randy's name, we all vouched for him on that later, but Randy must have been looking at us and not at Mike. So, the rock clobbered his leg.

Randy went down hard, howling.

This fortunate break allowed Chris and me to resume our quest. I grabbed the crystal and, seeing Mike coming my way, called out to Chris. I held the rock to my side, just like I'd seen Don Drysdale do on TV and pointed. I tossed the rock perfectly to Chris, who caught it with only a minor laceration, and the rock-throwing club was born.

This was how Chris and I invented the club. At first, toss-and-catch keep-away was our only activity. But soon we added other events, including the shot put for rocks too big to easily toss, and the round-rock discus—our way of skipping stones on dry land.

Life went on happily for several days. Word of our Rock Club spread, and gradually the second graders no longer had to order us all off the monkey bars. You'd have thought this would have made them happy, but no, they started coming out to see what we were doing out by the fence. Susan May, captain of the second-grade thugs, wanted a piece of the action. She wanted to take possession of our prized crystal.

"Let me see it," Susan May demanded.

"No!" all the first-grade boys said in unison.

"Give it to me, or I'll tell," she said.

We all looked at each other and shrugged. We weren't doing anything wrong.

"Susan May, your hair's like hay. You're slow as a snail. So go on and tattletale," I said, impressing everyone with my impromptu alliteration.

I thought she'd slink away in embarrassment. Instead she scowled, stomped her second-grade foot and crossed her second-grade arms. She was used to getting what she wanted, and was not about to budge.

"I'm not kidding," she said, and stuck out her tongue.

"Oooh, are we scared," Mike said. He was holding the crystal, and not about to give it up to a girl, even if she was a second-grader. We were savoring the moment. Let the second-graders have their monkey-bars. We had our rocks.

Then, Susan May narrowed her eyes at us and an evil grin spread across her face. We watched as she ran over to Mrs. Reyes, the playground monitor, and pointed our way. The recess bell rang, and we dropped the rocks, covered the best one with a quick kick in the dirt, and shuffled over towards our room.

Until we were nabbed by Mrs. Reyes.

"What were you boys doing over there?" she asked.

Mike, Chris, and Randy all looked my way, and then Mrs. Reyes' eyes locked on me.

"Nothing," I said, and then remembering my manners, "Nothing, ma'am."

"That is not what I hear." She gave me a look I'd seen all too often. She wanted a confession, but what was there to confess?

"Do we need to go to Mr. Lewis' office to discuss this?" she asked.

Now, there's a theory of evolution that says some animals develop instincts that help them survive. This is called "adaptive behavior." Apparently Chris, Mike and Randy had this in their genes. They *all* said, in perfect unison, "No! We're sorry and it won't happen again!" But there I was, like the kid still standing when the musical-chairs record stopped.

Mrs. Reyes stared at me.

"Well?" she asked. "What do *you* have to say about this?"

I thought hard and fast. What could you say about this problem? Finally, I came up with a great answer.

"Well, I think that there are lots of rocks on the playground and that Susan May ought to go find her own instead of bothering us."

This must not have been the answer Mrs. Reyes was looking for. Later, in the principal's office, Mr. Lewis' explained to me that sometimes when you are asked a question, it is better to keep quiet. He said: "If you can't say something nice, it is better not to say anything at all." He also said that my reason was a "poor excuse for my behavior."

Mr. Lewis didn't seem all that interested in the rocks, at least not the first time we met to discuss the Rock-Throwing Club. He told me that I needed to apologize for my remarks to Mrs. Reyes and to Susan May. I asked him what he wanted me to say, and he said that all true apologies "must come from the heart, and I can't tell you what you need to say."

He led me over to the little desk by the big green door,

and he gave me two pieces of paper on which to write my two apology notes. I sat there a long time and tried to find the right words. Finally, I knew what it was Mr. Lewis would want me to say, so I wrote two notes.

"Dear Mrs. Reyes: I am sorry I talked with you."

The first note took a long time, but then I got the hang of this apology-writing thing. The next note was much easier. I thought about what Susan May had demanded, and what we'd done. I knew right away what I'd do differently, if only given that second chance.

"Dear Susan May: I am sorry I didn't throw the rock at you."

When I was done, I gave the two notes to Mrs. Earl, the school secretary, and she read them. Her eyes got real big, and she made some choking sounds before she buzzed Mr. Lewis. She wiped her eyes and handed the notes to him. He looked at them both for a long, long time and then looked at me for an even longer time.

"Hmmmn. This is it, then?"

"Yes, sir!"

"It's what's in your heart?" He sighed, and put the papers on the counter-top.

I had a sinking feeling. Maybe I had misspelled something. But, I remembered what Mr. Lewis had just told me: "If you can't say something nice…." So, I decided to try this out and not say anything, but I smiled my best smile.

He looked at me and shook his head. "OK, Robb. That's all for now." Mr. Lewis put the notes in a big red folder with my name on it. He then scribbled a note to my teacher, and checked the box "excused absence." His note read:

"Please allow Robb to return to class."

So, I bounced down the echoing hallways to Room 2, and I handed the principal's note to my teacher. She frowned, and looked down at me over her glasses. She motioned for me to retake my seat at the back of the classroom, but for the first time I noticed something in her squinty eyes and clenched teeth, and I realized that Mrs. Reyes and I shared some things in common. We'd both been forced to accept excuses that didn't really cut it, and we both would be much happier if the stork *did* take back rejects on their return trip.

eight

TRICKS AND TREATS

I stood behind my mother waving a steak knife.

"Can I carve my own pumpkin?" I asked.

Mom turned away from the stove and disarmed me in one fluid motion.

"What's the rule about knives?" she said, frowning.

"Mom. I'm in the fourth grade now."

"So, you should know the rule by heart."

"I'm old enough to carve my own Jack-o-Lantern."

Mom wrapped a daisy-shaped hot pad around the blade. It was her turn to wave the knife at me, handle-out, of course.

"You're the oldest, and you need to set an example."

I sighed.

"OK, OK," I said "Your knife is not a toy. You're allowed to use it because you're a big boy."

"And?" Mom asked.

"You touch it when you have meat to cut. That's its only use, and nothing but."

"Right," Mom nodded.

"But… I've got a pumpkin." I pointed to the biggest, baddest, and most beautiful pumpkin that had ever come to rest on our yellow drop-leaf table. I walked over and

38

spun it slowly around, letting Mom see its perfection from every side.

"Wow," Mom said, and then looked at me with a raised eyebrow. "Looks like one of Mrs. Mallory's prize pumpkins." She nodded admiringly.

"She gave it to me," I said.

"Oh really," Mom again looked at me with wide eyes.

"Yeah, I raked her lawn," I explained.

"You offered to do that?"

"Not exactly." I chewed on my lip. I hadn't expected Mom to quiz me on how I'd gotten the pumpkin. I thought she'd just be happy to have it.

"So, she asked you to help?" Mom took off her apron, and sat down next to the pumpkin. She looked at me, her eyes flicking slightly from side to side, as if there was something that was crawling across my face.

"No. Not exactly," I said.

"Well, then, what exactly did happen?"

"Mrs. Mallory saw that the leaves were all scattered, and handed me a rake," I said. "Really, Mom. That's exactly what happened."

Mom thought about this for a while, and stared at the pumpkin.

"Why do I get the feeling that there's a part of this story missing?"

"You mean, like how the leaves fell off the tree?"

"I mean, why a polite woman like Mrs. Mallory would shove a rake into your hand without so much as a please or thank you." Mom smiled.

"Oh, well," I stroked the pumpkin. "It may be that I was standing in her yard."

"Standing?" Mom smiled quizzically.

"Jumping, actually," I said.

"Jumping?" Mom said. I watched the "little boat of her smile," as she called it in our Sunday-school songs, turn upside down.

"I guess I was jumping in a pile of leaves."

"You walked over and jumped in a pile of leaves she'd raked up?"

"I kind of dove into them."

"Dove?"

"And kicked."

Mom stood up, and paced back and forth in the kitchen. "And so you took this pumpkin from her?"

"Honest, Mom. She gave it to me."

So it was that Mom learned of how I'd been told to fix the mess I'd made, and then drafted into raking the rest of her front yard and back yard. At first, it was embarrassing—some of my friends came by and saw me working. But then, after I'd cleaned up the one pile, and made another for good measure, Mrs. Mallory let me start using the special wheeled leaf-sweeper. It was fun. I raced up and down the lawn, leaves flying into the catch-bag, and I piled bag after bag of red and yellow Sycamore leaves.

As I told my story, Mom quit pacing, sat down, and laughed at the description of "the biggest pile of leaves that anyone had ever seen."

"I guess you really did earn this pumpkin," Mom said.

"So can I carve it?"

"Do you think you can?" she asked.

I looked at the pumpkin, and the knife, and then at Mom.

"Yep."

"So," Mom asked, "What sort of scary face are you going to draw on it?"

I thought for a moment, and said, "I can't decide. Either Mrs. Mallory's face when I climbed out of the leaf pile ... or yours just now when you were standing at the stove."

nine

THE THREE O'CLOCK AROMA

Susan May knew how to tell it like it is.

"Boys stink!"

She stood in the center of the playground and shouted this to the world at large, tearing a hole in the peace of the Monday afternoon recess. She then wrinkled her nose and let her tongue poke slightly through her teeth.

There was a circle of five boys on the playground within spitting distance of Susan May. We looked at one another, not sure if the remark was a statement of fact or her philosophy of life. I was standing downwind of her. So I was pretty sure that it wasn't directed at me. But all five of us stopped, and waited to see what came next. Sam did look a bit red in the face. He was the nearest to her, and Sundays were often burrito nights over at his place. So, he was a prime suspect for a silent but deadly fragrance.

But there was no follow-up commentary. Susan May just stalked off in disgust. No one saw where she went, but it must have been a well-ventilated place that didn't allow boys.

Curious, I walked over to Sam. "What happened?" I asked.

"Beats me." Sam was admitting to nothing. "She was

41

reading a note or something."

Now Susan May did have something in her hands, but I didn't get a close look. Sam was clearly attempting to deflect attention from himself.

"You sure?" By this time the other three guys had all gathered around. It was late in the day, and we all were more or less covered in sweat and grime. Still, no one smelled particularly bad, and Sam swore that he didn't break wind. We were mystified, and after the bell rang we returned for the final hour in class none the wiser.

This was on my mind as the final bell rang, and when I got home I saw Dad in the driveway. He was working split shifts in the oilfields, and was tinkering with the lawn mower.

"Dad. Do I smell?" I asked.

"And how," he nodded. "Your mother can never bake cookies without you showing up."

"Not like that," I rolled my eyes. "I mean do I, ah, *stink*?"

He looked me over, squinting at me as if he could gauge stink with his eyes.

"Probably," he said at last. "Who doesn't?"

"Oh." I hadn't expected this answer, not from Dad anyway. "Badly?" I asked.

"Well, no more than usual anyway," he said.

This was a bit better, but I still wanted something to use against Susan May to defend myself. I wondered if there was any way I could rank how rank I smelled.

"Do *you* stink?" I asked.

He thought about that, lifted his arm and smelled the pit. He winced dramatically, but then grinned.

"Not at all."

I waited for some elaboration. But he went back to the lawnmower. I walked over to him, and he was drenched in sweat, and smelled like a mixture of gasoline, Lucky Strikes, and Danny, the terrier next door. He noticed that I was sniffing the air.

"So, do you think I stink?" he asked.

"Sorta," I said softly.

"*Ha!*" he slapped his pants and startled me. "That's *man smell*. It's what a guy is supposed to smell like."

Mom had walked out into the driveway to bring Dad some ice water, and she heard the tail end of our conversation.

"Man smell?" she said.

"Yeah," Dad said, his swagger now in a lower gear.

"Right." She looked at me. "That's the smell a man gives off right before he's told he's going to have to shower outside—with the hose."

I decided, compared to Dad, I must not smell all that bad. So I asked Mom what she thought.

"Well, step over here away from your father."

I did as I was told. Mom walked over to me, put her hands on me and closed her eyes, inhaling deeply, much as a faith healer might.

"You've got the Three O'clock Aroma," she said with an air of authority.

"Do you mean I'm sweaty?"

"Boys don't sweat," she said automatically. "They perspire. *Animals* sweat."

Now, this was news to me. We lived in Oildale. Summers often topped 105 degrees, and I thought I'd been sweating the better part of my whole life.

"Do women sweat?"

"Certainly not," she said. "Women *glow*."

Dad laughed, and stood up. He wiped the perspiration from his face, and walked over towards Mom, arms outstretched.

"Hey glow worm. How about a hug?"

Mom took a step back, and wrinkled her nose just like Susan May.

"No, thanks." She sat the water down on the driveway, and walked briskly back into the house.

I watched her go, still unsure if I smelled or not. Dad

was putting away his tools, ready to tackle the lawn.

"What's the 'Three O'clock Aroma'?" I asked.

"Oh, that." He scratched behind his ear. "That's when you smell OK enough to run an errand… or mow the lawn… but not good enough to go to church."

Suddenly, I no longer cared all that much if I smelled. I could see that my afternoon freedom was now on the line, the result of asking one too many questions.

"Thanks," I said, and raced towards the house.

"Where you going?" Dad shouted.

"Gonna take a shower—just to be sure." I was inside before he had a chance to say any more.

So in the 5th grade I learned the difference between sweat and perspiration, but I'm still not sure about "glow." I also learned that cleanliness may not exactly be next to godliness, but a well-timed hot shower beats mowing the lawn any day.

ten

SIGNS OF TROUBLE

The highlight of our summer was when Mom and Dad packed up our Pontiac station wagon and headed for Pismo Beach. Mom loaded the car with diversions, such as coloring books and road-sign bingo cards, but she knew that these wouldn't hold us for the entire trip. So she made sure that our seating strategy was designed to increase our chances of reaching the beach alive. My sister Pat sat in the front seat with Mom and Dad, my brother Jim sat in the middle seat next to all the food, and I was in the rearward-facing seat in back with all the luggage.

For years Mom told me that this was a special seat that not just anyone could use on a long trip. For example, they tried putting Jim back there, and he got carsick before we even got out of town. This pretty much took the edge off *that* ride. So I was elected to hold down the luggage, and I never puked. Not once. At the time, I thought of it as a major life achievement for a 10-year-old. Mom often commented on how well I did in the all-the-way-back seat. Only later did I hear that Mom decided I needed to be in back because it was the best way to keep me and Dad as far apart as possible in such a small place. She was trying to avoid trouble, but all she did was move trouble to the back seat.

The rear set had one drawback: I had to crawl over all

the food, my brother, and the luggage to get in and out of the car. But the way-back seat did have its perks. It gave me an interesting view of the world. I got to watch where we'd been and the satisfaction of knowing that we were leaving. This was a nice feeling when we were putting miles between us and a place like Bakersfield. Since the back seat faced to the rear, everyone else in my family was facing the other direction and not paying all that much attention to me. I got to gawk at people who drove by, and I had a variety of games I used to play on tailgaters— people who got close enough to get a really good look.

One of my favorite things to do was to hold up a realistic toy gun and look at the driver menacingly. This caused some people to back off—mostly those with East Coast license plates. One time, though, a guy in a one-ton flatbed with Texas plates reached back and pulled his shotgun off the rack and sat it on his dash, the two barrels trained on me. He grinned, but he also followed us for mile after mile with that thing pointed at me.

That was the last time I did the pistol trick.

Still, there were other diversions. Another favorite pastime was to make signs and hold them up to the rear window. The signs might say helpful things like "Pass Carefully, Driver Chewing Tobacco." You could tell who believed this because they'd drop way back, and wait miles and miles for a passing lane. Other signs contained taunts: "We may Be Slow—But We're Ahead of You!" This often prompted just the opposite effect of the Chew-Signs; the driver would scowl, squint, and then pass in the face of oncoming traffic. They'd cut Dad off. This usually spurred an outpouring of colorful language from my father, who wanted to chase the offenders down, until my Mom restrained him and reminded him that an overloaded station wagon is not a police interceptor. Still, Dad would yell, *"Get that license number!"* But Mom never did.

The art of the back seat car sign is to hold it up long enough to be seen by the driver behind us but not by Dad in his rearview mirror or Mom during her periodic head count to see if someone had climbed onto the rear bumper.

I was the master of the sleight-of-sign, and my backseat shenanigans were undetected for years, until I decided it would be fun to try something new.

Before this trip, my Mom fretted about a big story in the newspaper. Some crazy woman who wanted to have kids—but couldn't. Mom couldn't quit talking about it, and finally I asked her what "abducted" meant, and she said that it meant "kidnapped," when someone took a child that wasn't theirs without the parents' knowledge. Mom repeated her oft-told warning of not wandering off with strangers.

Dad wasn't worried. He'd tried to give me away a couple of time, but he'd had no takers. Even so, Mom took the precaution of stenciling our names and phone numbers in our underwear and jackets.

But this got me to thinking. It would be a great fun to make up a new sign that said: "HELP! I've been kidnapped. Call the police." This was a lot of information to write on one sign, and so the lettering was pretty small. I wasn't sure if kidnapped was one word or two, so I had to look it up it the dictionary I brought on the trip. I worked carefully with my crayons and markers to fit all the words on my cardboard sign, and I couldn't wait to try it out.

My first victim was a bald guy who was driving a pickup. He frowned for a minute, and then just laughed, waved, and honked as he drove by.

I guess he figured out the gag.

Most of the other people I tried had similar reactions. Then I tried it on a white haired old lady driving a VW. She looked at the sign, and seemed confused. I saw her reach down in her purse and pull out a pair of glasses. She put them on, looked at me again, and looked startled. The head bobbed up and down as she nodded, and then made slashing downward motions with her hand, followed us closely to the next exit, and then peeled off. I lost sight of her as she dove into a gas station.

I decided that the sign was a bust, and lost interest. So, I picked up a Hardy Boys book, and burrowed down in the luggage to read for a while.

About 15 minutes later, something odd happened. I heard a siren, and I looked up to see not one, but two police cars had surrounded our wagon, boxing us in and forcing us to pull over.

Dad swore.

"What's wrong?" Mom asked.

"Damned if I know," Dad said.

The officers advanced on both sides, guns drawn. Mom looked back and squealed.

"Don't move!" a cop yelled. And Dad didn't move. Then the cop looked at my brother, sister and me and frowned.

"Are you kids OK?" the cop asked.

"I have to go to the bathroom," Pat said. "I'm hungry," Jim added. I realized what was happening, and slid the signs behind the ice chest. "I didn't do it," I said helpfully.

"Do what?" Mom asked, taking over the police work.

The cops lowered their guns, reassessing the situation.

"Step out of the car, please Ma'am," said the officer nearest my mom, holstering his weapon. The other stood in a strategic position, next to the driver's door. Dad sat silently and stared straight ahead, his jaw muscles pulsating.

The cop walked my mother to the back of the car, and she opened the tailgate at his direction. All my signs, wedged between the ice chest and the door, tumbled out on the ground at their feet. Mom looked at them, and then at me, wide-eyed.

The officer gathered up my messages. "Son, did you make these?" he asked, his lips pursed.

"Yes sir."

There was a long silence. He scanned the car, looking

us all up and down.

"Is this your mother?"

"Yes sir," I whispered.

The officer nodded his head and jerked his thumb towards the front of the car.

"And who is that man?"

I looked at my father. The other patrolman still had his gun in hand, and stood just inches from Dad. My father was facing him, hands in plain view on the steering wheel. I could only see the back of Dad's head and neck, which were a bright red. I shifted my view to the rear-view mirror, and I could see the expression on his face. His mouth no longer had teeth; they were gritted fangs.

My voice failed me altogether.

The officer rested his free hand on his holster, which was still unsnapped.

"Son, you can tell me the truth." The officer smiled, cocked his head, and then motioned towards Dad.

"Is this man your father?"

In the rear view mirror, I saw Dad's lips move silently. I couldn't make out what he was saying, but it didn't seem to be "I love you."

I drew a deep breath, but only a squeak came out. "He was…."

The officer nodded, and waved off the other patrolman. I saw my father let go of the steering wheel, but his color changed from red to the sort of purple that Mom wore on Easter.

This didn't look good to me.

The patrolman bent down on one knee, and seemed twice as big up close. "So, son," he drummed his fingers on the signs and squinted at me. "Do you realize how serious this is?"

"I think so," I said, my voice still barely a squeak.

He leaned even closer, eyes fixed on mine, and waited. I exercised the right to remain silent. Then Mom jumped in on my behalf.

"Oh, officer, I can assure you we'll take care of this."

"DAMN STRAIGHT!" my father said, firing off his first words on the subject. "He'll get it, all right."

I swallowed involuntarily.

The officer looked away from me and my multi-colored father, shuffled through my signs, reading each one in turn. He slowly straightened the signs, and again looked at me, his eyes dancing. "And what do you have to say for yourself?" he asked, in a softer tone.

"Sorry?" I looked again at my father who nodded his head curtly in agreement.

"Won't do it again?" the officer asked helpfully, biting his lip.

"No sir, never."

He put his face close to mine, and whispered, "Cross your heart?"

I silently crossed my heart, terror in my eyes.

He stood up, looked at my father's contorted face in the mirror, and then leaned over near my mother and whispered something in her ear.

"No, that won't be necessary," she said, and to my surprise, she smiled. "I'll take care of it."

"Very well, then," the patrolman responded and nodded. "I don't think you'll need these anymore." He tucked the signs under his arm, and left.

Mom got back into the car, and then she whispered something in Dad's ear, and kissed him on the cheek. He frowned, and we drove onward in subdued silence.

I wasn't sure how to read the mood in the front seat. What was "it?" I had long heard Dad say "YOU'RE GOING TO GET 'IT.'" Mom had even promised the patrolman that she was going to take care of 'it.' Now, I was afraid, I was finally going to find out.

I hunkered down in the back seat, unable to read or do much of anything. It was a long, long way to the next gas station. I waited until Dad had gone inside to pay, and I scrambled over the seat to talk to Mom.

I sat down next to her and peered searchingly into her face.

"Do you need to use the restroom?" she asked nonchalantly.

"No."

"Well, then, you'd better get back in your seat."

"OK," I said, but I lingered.

She looked at me, amused. "So...what now?"

"Mom, what is *it*?"

"It?"

"*What did the policeman say?*"

"Oh, that." She smiled. "He was a bit worried about you."

"Yeah?"

"He offered to take you in his patrol car."

"Take me?" I was shocked. "He was going to arrest me?"

"No, love," she laughed, pinched my chin, and nudged me to return to the back seat. "He was offering '*protective custody*.'"

eleven

GETTING IN & OUT OF HOT WATER
9 HELPFUL HINTS

In grade school I was considered a problem child and spent hours and hours in the principal's outer office. I was there so often that they had to bring in a second desk, devoted more-or-less to me and a few of my best friends.

The problem was that I *loved* to talk, and I assumed that whatever interested me just *had* to interest everyone else. I was proud of all the things I learned from reading and was determined to share. I mean, if it's important enough to be in the *World Book*, shouldn't everyone hear about it?

Apparently not. This leads to **_Hint #1: only a few people want to be enlightened. Most folks just want to be left alone._**

So the talking-in-class thing bought me numerous tickets to the big green door of Mr. Lewis' office.

I was in hot water so often that I should have brought swim trunks to school.

But that wouldn't have helped me on one occasion, showing off some new words I'd just learned. I used them, and was promptly sent to the boys' bathroom to wash my mouth out with *soap* —they made a classmate come and watch—and *then* I had to talk with Mr. Lewis. This is hard to do when your tongue is numb.

But at least they let me use *cold* water.

Mr. Lewis' helpful **Hint #2: Don't use words you can't find in the dictionary**. Or, as Mom told me later "Just because an adult uses a word doesn't mean *you* can."

But of all my misdeeds, the Rock-Throwing Club bought me the most trips to see Mr. Lewis. At the start, it was supposed to be a secret, but we drew a cult following. It began as a small-scale activity, just me and a few buddies trying to amuse ourselves. But we couldn't keep it away from the other kids. For a brief while, everyone wanted in on the act. Then things got ugly, and we were shut down—forced to go underground.

Still, I think it wasn't *my fault* that other people caused trouble. After all, nobody got hurt. Well, not much anyway. My friends and I were just minding our own business.

Really.

For the record. I never did aim at, or much less hit anyone with so much as a marshmallow. The rocks were handy because I couldn't bring a baseball to school, and I made a point of being way-far-away from the others. This was especially true when my buddies and I were scolded. They gave it all up, but I persisted. I hung out near the fence, tossing rocks and watching them fly.

I don't know why this was so pleasurable, but it was. I never made it to the majors, but I was regularly sent up to the office.

To try and break me of this *terrible habit*, Mr. Lewis tried something called behavior modification. This apparently involves galvanized-steel buckets and leather work gloves. I was forced to go out and pick up bucket after bucket of rocks, and then bring them back to the office.

Mr. Lewis was determined to ruin my pitching arm. I

had to forgo throwing and was lugging a bazillion buckets to and fro.

I'm not sure what he did with all these rocks. Chris thought he was probably selling them on the black market.

But because of all this grade-school community service, I spend many solitary afternoons out on the 1st -3rd graders' playground, gathering a trillion tons of rocks.

At first, it was hard, but by the time I hit 4th grade, it was *much* easier to pick up the rocks. Mr. Lewis had provided me with a do-it-yourself Charles Atlas bodybuilding program. But this eventually ended when I simply could not find any more rocks. My four years of rock-collecting had stripped the place of rocks and pebbles alike. There was nothing left on the playground bigger than a grain of sand. So, **Hint #3: You can survive your problems, if you're willing to outlast the opposition**.

So, was I reformed by pounding rocks?

Nope.

Without rocks, I took up other pursuits. Undaunted, I turned to *paper* projectiles.

In short order, I was caught flicking spit wads across the room. But this was done in the name of science.

Really.

No malice intended, I was simply studying geometry, mathematics, and momentum. I was a student of the comparative physical properties of paper-and-spittle pellets verses gum-infused paper-wads. I even tested various types of gum, ranging from Wrigley's to Hubba-Bubba and even the appropriately named Bazooka bubble gum. One day I wondered if it was possible to get a piece of paper from one end of the classroom to the other and the next I was manning the artillery. The rest, as they say, is histrionics.

But before I was shut down, I did make a semi-major discovery: chewing gum has the more consistent trajectory and greater range, but travels *much* slower and more conspicuously to target.

It was the chewing gum that got me sent to the

principal's office for a bonus-round enhanced consequence. This time I was handed a green wastebasket with the number seven stenciled on its side. I pondered the meaning of this.

Was spit balling one of the seven deadly sins?

Was I about to get punished "Seven Ways to Sunday" as my father so often told me?

Again, the answer was not so mysterious; it was that this bucket was supposed to remain in room seven. I was sent there to lie under desks and scrape gum, which is actually not as bad as it sounds.

Really.

I think they stopped when they realized that I found this interesting. There are a million kinds of gum, and they create a zillion interlocking patterns when smashed.

Fascinating. You should check it out sometime.

Hint #4: Some punishments are more *interesting* than you'd think. Especially when compared to having your mouth washed out with industrial-strength soap.

***

Alas, school wasn't the only place where I felt the heat. It happened at home, too. But I learned that the best way to stay out of trouble was to stay *outside*.

Usually.

The hope is that whatever goes awry might escape the watchful eyes of my mother.

Hint #5: Remember that having an adventure is like buying a home. What matters the most is location, location, location.

In reality, though, this doesn't always work. My mom, like most mothers, has atomic X-ray super-vision. She can see through walls, the blackness of night, and detect what was happening in the trees and our neighbors' backyards miles away.

Another hint: This is the *crucial* difference between

mothers and fathers.

I could start a fire in the front room, lighting a road flare over a trash can, and my father will *not* notice so long as I didn't do it directly between the color TV and his Barcalounger.

Mom will *know* even if she was shopping, ten miles away.

She also has Mom-telepathy. She'd know I was *about* to get into trouble before anything happened. Even when I have great ideas, like drying my model airplanes in the oven, Mom can stop me before I get a chance to burn the house down.

Usually, it worked like this. I'll be absorbed in a project idea—not bothering *anyone*—and I'll wander out to the backyard or garage (if Dad isn't around). I'll stare at the workbench or tools, having genius-ideas, when she would show up and spoil everything.

Take the time I was ready to make my own industrial-strength slingshot. I was in the garage, scoping out supplies.

Out of nowhere, Mom appeared and asked, "What'cha you up to?"

"Nothing," I said. And this was true because I actually hadn't *started* making it yet.

"Uh—huh." She raised her eyebrows and tapped her foot. Then she stood there and just watched me.

This made it pretty much impossible to think.

"You're not thinking of using that elastic tubing Dad bought?"

"Is that rubber?" I said, answering her question with a question.

Hint #6: Total honesty is often the best policy, especially when you can still be misleading.

When asked a question, answer with a question. Yes, this is *always* the best way to dodge a direct question. Unless your mother went to the same school mine did.

"So, you *were* thinking of using it," she said, ignoring

my question.

"*I didn't say that,*" I mumbled, but I knew there wasn't much point in denying it.

"Don't," Mom said. "Find something productive to do."

"OK, OK," I said, "I won't touch the tubing. And I wasn't going to use much of it, anyway."

"Good," she nodded, and I saw her look over in the corner of the garage, where the rakes and brooms were stored.

"The driveway could use sweeping."

"Maybe when I get back from Chris'," I replied as I dashed across the floor and grabbed my bicycle.

She shrugged, and I pedaled off. Sometimes she'd be satisfied just to have me doing my thing over at Chris'. At least when things went south, it wasn't on *her* watch or her turf. And his parents were much less suspicious than mine.

Hint #7: Choose friends with nearsighted parents.

***

Still, I did get into trouble before Mom could stop me.

To obtain forgiveness, I'd have to square things with Mom. As I got older, I usually knew, right after I had done something that knocked the garage door off its hinges or set off a smoke alarm that I was going to get it.

When Dad got home.

But if I could win Mom over, keep her goodwill between Dad's wrath and my hide, things would usually work out reasonably well.

And when it came to placating Mom, there was really only one surefire way out: *preemptive housework.*

The idea behind preemptive housework was to "pick a corner, and just clean." That was Mom's standard approach to cleaning an area, usually my bedroom, which looked like it ought to be just sealed off and condemned. I found it's better to clean up a *family area* like the kitchen. I learned this by chance one day when trying to hide the fact that I'd accidently eaten about half a bag of sugar.

How can you accidently eat half a bag?

Well, silly, it is because the other half of the bag exploded when you dropped it from the top shelf of the cupboard in a direct hit on the coffee kettle on the stove. I cleaned that stove, and the counter, and the floor, and the windowsill and the drawers I'd pulled open to climb up. I cleaned and cleaned. I'd hoped that my feasting and bombardment would go unnoticed, but it didn't. My mother was so deeply moved and *grateful* that someone, for once, had cleaned the kitchen that she hugged me and found my face to be sticky. I'd forgotten to clean that. But the best part was she didn't care. *Not at all.* She was in ecstasy that someone had cleaned up, and *it wasn't her.*

Hint #8: The way to a woman's heart is to *clean the kitchen.*

And that's what I did for much of my childhood. When I'd break a window, I'd clean the kitchen. When I found out what happens when you throw Salvo tablets into the pool, I cleaned the kitchen. Once in a while, I cleaned the kitchen before I went out, just in case.

This was *usually* a great idea.

There are exceptions to everything, and the exception to the cleaning-is-great-rule came one day when I was looking for a good deed to do, and looked just beyond the kitchen to the front room. The front room was forbidden territory, for company only. Funny thing was we never had any company that was entertained there. Maybe we were saving it for a visit from the Pope or the President, but we never went in there. So, it was a beautiful but unused and dusty place.

Dusty. Now that was something I could do something about. I looked at the dust, and I noticed that there was an entire shelf dedicated to my mother's finest crystal, stuff she'd inherited. There was a row of large goblets, caked in so much dust that the rims of them were all brown.

So, I carefully crawled up and brought down all one dozen of them, and since I didn't have a lot of time, I put them all in our dishwasher. They were too tall to fit on the top shelf, but I managed to wedge them, or most of them, oh-so-carefully, into the bottom shelf.

Mom always said "don't go for half-measures," and I'd made this my personal credo. I set all the controls for pot scrub and extra heat, and I poured in tons and tons of soap. I was determined to make this dusty, brown-encrusted crystal sparkle. Mom was going to be so proud. I figured I was as good as gold for being able to fuss for outrageous toys or just have a bit of cushion in the "problem" department. I was polishing my halo.

Alas, it didn't work out that way. Mark Twain once noted that "all that glitters is not gold." Sadder still, he said, "gold itself is a rather dull looking thing in its natural state." It is, as I can tell you with *absolute* authority on this matter, a rather cruddy-looking brown.

But it wasn't Mark Twain who taught me this lesson. No, I learned it when my mother walked by her crystal goblet collection—her once covered with gold leaf crystal—and stopped so fast that she just about tripped on the shag carpeting, and just stood staring, like she was watching some sort of tornado coverage on television. The only other time I'd seen this particular expression was when she and I were watching old news footage of the Hindenburg disaster. Mom opened her mouth, but nothing came out, and I thought for a minute that she was speechless with joy.

"Who? Who?" was all she could manage, sounding something like an owl.

"I knew you'd be surprised," I beamed, and Mom leaned against me and began to cry. This seemed pretty ridiculous. I knew she had to be happy, but sobbing? Wow. Score one for Robb!

"You washed the crystal?" she asked, gasping between each syllable.

"Yep!" I replied.

"How? How?" she hooted.

"Pot scrub, extra-hot water, and a double-douse of Electrosol..."

"Why? Why?" Mom looked at the ceiling as she asked this last question, so I wasn't sure that she was asking me or talking to God. But I decided I'd better answer, since there was no one else in the room.

"They were dirty," I said, "and I'd run out of things to do."

Mom looked stunned, apparently overcome with joy, because she dropped her journalistic investigation and retired to the front room, where she went to lay down on the couch.

I was mostly pleased with myself, having gotten almost all of the crystal in. Oddly, though, Mom later hid those still-unwashed pieces from me.

Never did know what became of them.

I guess she figured I'd been so helpful, she'd take care of them herself.

Later, when she'd composed herself, she came in and gave me a hug. She still teared up, but she only said that "some things are not meant to go in the dishwasher. They just can't stand the hot water."

So, even when trying to do good, I can still manage to get in hot water.

But I didn't get punished. That day I saw with clarity, that the *real* gold was in Mom's heart. Even when I was screwing up, she still saw through it all to my good intentions.

Even now, I *do* still try to have more good days than bad, and make Mom proud.

Hint #9: Good deeds *do* go unpunished.

twelve

SOONER OR LATER

I thought I'd include a couple of stories focused on my parents, so you can see where I get my quirks....

My mother's motto is: "Don't put off until tomorrow that which you can do today." She said this often, but mostly she taught by example.

For instance, one morning she decided that we needed a clock in the dining room, and before noon, she'd purchased a brand-new, bright red Telechron wall clock. Dad was home from the oilfields for lunch, so she asked him to hang it.

"Whatta ya need that for?" Dad asked through a mouthful of tuna fish sandwich. He flipped open the box and looked suspiciously at the plastic timepiece. "The grandfather clock is in the front room."

"I can't see it from the table," Mom said.

"So, walk around the corner," Dad offered helpfully.

Mom pursed her lips.

Dad sighed. "How many clocks do you need around here, anyway?" he asked.

"I'm tired of people showing up late for dinner," Mom

61

said. "We need a clock in here."

Dad looked at her for a long minute, or so it seemed. Without a second hand to refer to, it was hard to tell. He chewed on what was left of his sandwich, trying to untangle the logic of how a wall clock in the dining room would suddenly make people on time.

Dad shuffled through the remains of the morning paper. Clearly, this was one of those arguments that the person who spoke next was bound to lose. He looked again at the clock, contemplating the project at length, as a surgeon might review an X-ray.

"Oh come on," Mom said. "It'll just take a second."

Dad knew better than to argue. Arguments were usually more trouble than the project. But I could tell that he was not eager to take this on. He scrunched his face up and looked at the clock.

"You like this color?"

Mom opened her eyes wide. "Spoken by the man who will wear a red shirt with green socks."

The standoff was broken when the grandfather clock struck half past, and Dad glanced at his battered Timex. "Gotta run."

"The clock?" Mom asked.

"Can't now."

"When?" she pressed.

"Sooner or later," he said, and tried to kiss Mom on the cheek, but she dodged him.

"Later, then," she said.

Dad was gone, and Mom stomped out into the garage and looked at Dad's tool bench. This was a sacred space that I knew well to leave alone. But Mom had the advantage of being an adult, and the power that comes from being really "teed off." She studied the wall, and found what she was looking for, a hammer. It was a ball-peen hammer, but a hammer nonetheless. She grabbed it, and rummaged through the cabinet next to the bench. Mom took the first box of nails she found. They were the size of railroad spikes.

"Will those work?" I wondered aloud.

"Nails are nails," she said coolly. "You won't see it anyway, if you think about it."

I had to admit she was right about that. It was going to be behind the clock. It took Mom all of two minutes to hang the clock.

"I don't know why he made such a fuss about this," Mom said.

The first problem arose when she tried to plug in the clock, and realized the cord was too short to reach the outlet. I watched silently, and she removed the clock from the wall, smiling brightly.

"No problem, it will look just fine over here." She moved the clock a bit closer to the outlet, and pounded in another spike.

This, too, proved to be not quite close enough, and Mom had to pound yet one more nail in place. "Third try's a charm."

Mom then went into the garage and brought out a crow bar to remove the oversize nails. She managed to remove the first one, only denting the wall slightly. The second nail must have found its way into a wooden stud, and she punched a hole in the wall right next to the nail, without so much as budging the spike.

"Well," Mom said. "Well hell."

I was shocked, but not so much as when she grabbed a picture out of the closet and hung it on the spike, covering the hole. It was an out of sight, out of mind solution that I could relate to. It was how I approached cleaning my room.

Mom still had to deal with the electric cord. It did reach now, but it hung in an awkward corkscrew from the clock to the outlet.

"Hmm..." Mom said, as we both looked at the mess.

"Maybe Dad can fix this," I said.

Mom stiffened. "How hard can it be?" she said. Then

she went back to Dad's cabinet, this time taking her time to find just what she was looking for. She brought out a box of tacks and set them on the dining room table. She stretched the cord taught, tacks in hand, and began carefully tapping them directly through the electrical cord to keep in straight and tidy. Satisfied at last, she set the clock to the correct time and plugged it in.

The hands on the bright-red clock remained frozen, but the white power cord did begin to move. It twitched once or twice, straining against its constraints, and then began to actively smoke and shake, sizzling itself and the wall behind it into a charcoal shades of black and gray. Mom tried unplugging the cord, but it bit her, and she had to run to the garage and turn off the circuit breaker.

By the time Dad came home, the wires had quit smoking; but it took him a while longer to cool off.

He tackled the repair job after dinner, laying out a drop sheet and unpacking his tools. All the time he was shaking his head and muttering.

"Damn impatient woman."

The project took him the rest of the night, scraping melted wires off the wall, doing a proper wiring job, and then topping it all off with a fresh coat of paint.

When he was done, he stood back to admire his work, plugged in the little red clock, and watched it spring to life. Then he nodded, a smile of satisfaction creeping onto his face. He announced his accomplishment with a question posed, it seemed, to the clock itself.

"So, you just couldn't wait a bit?"

Mom watched at a safe distance, and when Dad began to pack up his tools, she brought him a cup of coffee and slipped her arm around him.

He looked at her and rolled his eyes. She tilted her head and smiled.

"You going to be mad at me forever?" she asked.

"I'm thinking about it."

"Oh, you'll get over it," Mom said confidently.

"And when will that happen?" Dad asked.

She kissed him on the cheek, and hugged him. "Oh, sooner or later."

thirteen

HOW A *MAN* DOES IT

Dad sauntered in from the garage and into the kitchen. He opened a cupboard and rummaged a bit, frowning.

"Hey, we're outta coffee!" Dad yelled. He was at the counter doing the one thing he was allowed to do in the kitchen: making the morning brew.

"I know," Mom said from the laundry room.

"Well…"

"Well what?" Mom said.

Dad stared at the coffee pot. He didn't do his best thinking in the morning. Even though it was Saturday, and his day off, he wasn't smiling.

"When?" he asked.

"When what?" Mom said.

Without coffee, Dad couldn't put a full sentence together. Half awake, he rubbed his stubble and blurted out: *"When in the Sam Hill are you buying coffee?"*

There was a long silence. It was one of those moments when the person who spoke next was going to lose the round. Mom marched from the laundry room, to their bedroom, and then back down the hallway to the kitchen.

She slammed her purse on the table, and gave Dad a withering look.

He averted her gaze.

"Here," she flung the checkbook across the table.

"Oh, no," Dad said, retreating.

"Oh, *yes.*" She continued digging in her purse. She produced her weekly shopping list, and the keys to the station wagon. She held them up in his face. Dad cringed like a vampire being shown a crucifix.

"Hey, that's *your* job," he said.

"I just retired." Mom forced the list into his hand, prying open his clenched fist. Her keys fell, rattling on the floor.

"Now, you're set." Mom gathered up her purse, smoothed her dress, and strode out of the room, head high.

"I'm not going," Dad said to her back, defeat in his voice.

"Then you're going to get mighty hungry this week."

"I don't know my way around…" he pleaded

"Perfect. Then you can take your son to help."

***

And that, as Mom was fond of saying, was that. Thirty minutes later, Dad and I were cruising the aisles of Safeway. It was the first time I remember seeing my father operate a shopping cart. The two front wheels wobbled uncooperatively, and he gritted his teeth as he fought to keep moving in a straight line.

"Want some help, Dad?"

"I can manage," he said, scowling.

"OK. But do you, ah," I hesitated, "Do you know what you're doing?"

He stopped, stiffened, and looked down on me. I saw fire in his eyes, and he got about a foot taller.

"Do I look like I need help?" he said. "Do you think I

can't do something that old women do?"

It occurred to me that Dad still hadn't had his morning cup of coffee, and I had better lie low until he did.

"OK kiddo, let me show you something. Watch closely. Today you'll see how a man does it."

With that, he bolted down the aisle and towards the cereal section. Without stopping, he grabbed boxes of Wheaties, corn flakes, and oatmeal, heaving each into the cart with a flick of his wrist.

I hustled to keep up.

"Mom always checks prices," I said.

"I'm not Mom," he said, and popped a wheelie past the Frosted Flakes.

Dad shopped the same way he drove—a take-no-prisoners method of getting from start to finish as fast as possible. Courtesy, the rules of the road, and even common sense were merely suggestions. If any of these threatened to make him spend even one instant longer in the hated grocery store, then they were circumvented or ignored.

We passed the dairy section without stopping.

"We're out of milk," I said.

"Not on the list." He tossed me Mom's notes.

I checked.

"But it says '1 gallon.'"

"Yeah, but it doesn't say a gallon of *what*, does it?"

He rounded another corner on two wheels.

"Hey, it could be a gallon of paint, chlorine, motor oil, or bubble bath. Right?"

I kept quiet. Man-logic, I guessed, is an acquired skill.

We did stop by the coffee section, and Dad loaded up with five cans of coffee.

"That'll last us a while," he said.

It wasn't exactly a lifetime supply, but it was enough to make sure that he wouldn't need to return for months, even if they dropped the A-Bomb. Mom, though, was not so lucky. Most of the items listed weren't purchased.

"What about all this other stuff?" I said, looking over dozens of items that Dad had skipped.

"No stupid piece of paper is bossing *me* around," he said, thumping his chest like Tarzan did when talking to Cheetah.

"Mom's not going to like this," I said.

"Tough," he said, squinting at me. "I. Am. Done."

And he was.

The cart had a handful of things he knew *he* needed: his favorite cereals, some shaving cream, razor blades, TP, beef jerky, and coffee, of course. Lots and lots of coffee. Normally a Saturday shopping run would fill two or three carts and up to a dozen bags.

We returned home, and Mom watched Dad carry in his purchases—two bags. I entered empty-handed.

"Where's the rest?" she asked.

"Got all we need here."

He plopped the stuff on the counter, pulling out all his MJB to form a coffee-can pyramid. Then he crossed his arms.

"And just for the record, I'm not going back there again," he said, pointing towards the store, "to do *your* work." He squared his shoulders and then sauntered off to the safety of his workshop.

Mom watched him go, looking at the bags, and then at me. She peeked in the one bag still on the counter, and shook her head.

"I told him to use the list," I said. "But he said that he was showing me 'How a Man Shops.'"

I was worried that she'd yell at me. Instead Mom sighed, smiled, and then winked.

"That's OK," she said, nodding. "He'll get the rest when he goes back."

"*Back to the store?*" I gasped.

"Mmm-hmmmm," Mom nodded, smoothing out her shopping list on the kitchen table.

"*Today?* Really?" I asked.

"Sooner than later," Mom replied.

I watched as she ran her finger down the list, grabbed a felt pen, and made some marks on the page. I peeked and saw that just under item #7 "coffee" was item #8 "filters." She circled it in red. And beside the circle she'd added three underlined words. "Finish Shopping Or ..."

"Or.... *What?*" I wondered.

Her note didn't say, but when I looked at Mom's face, and saw her jaw jut out, I decided I probably didn't want to know. Then a wonderful-terrible thought crossed my mind. Someone was in trouble, and it wasn't me.

What a relief!

Still, I waited with the sort of fascination you'd feel seeing a spider getting ready to eat a fly or reading Mad Magazine's latest *Spy verses Spy* episode. I watched Mom dart to the kitchen counter and grab a box by the coffeemaker. She extracted the last two filters.

And tossed them in the trash.

Empty box still in hand, she inserted her list, closed the lid, and nestled it artfully in front of Dad's coffee stockpile. She double-checked to make sure it was dead-center, making an aesthetically pleasing presentation. Even so, Mom's entire countermove operation had taken just seconds.

She stepped back and rubbed her hands together in satisfaction. Then she looked at me and arched her eyebrows.

"Now that, son," Mom said, "is how a *woman* does it."

fourteen

THE ENCYCLOPEDIA KID

I was in the back yard, lying on the ground and looking up. Mom was busy with the laundry.

"How come the sky is blue?" I asked.

Mom just finished hanging my Cub Scout uniform and answered, as best she could with a mouthful of clothespins.

"Because that's what color it is."

"But how come?" I asked.

"Because it is," she said.

"But *why?*"

"*Because,*" she said, her voice going up three octaves.

I could see where this line of questioning was heading, and knew I needed to change my approach.

"*Because* why?" I asked, trying to head her off. But without luck.

"*Just because,*" Mom said, tossing the remaining clothespins back into a coffee can hanging on the line. She walked back in the house and ended her participation in my scientific inquiry.

Often I'd bug mom with tough questions. When I

stumped her, rather than admit she didn't know, she had a standard set of low-impact answers:

"Because that's the way it's always been…."

"Because that's the way the world works…."

"Because that's God's will…."

"Just because…."

So later that day, I tried asking Dad this same question about the sky, and he told me "That's a silly question: It's blue because it's not red."

Gee thanks, Dad.

Dad loved to give me silly answers to what he called my "silly questions." When he didn't know the answer, he'd crack a joke or just make something up. But in a pinch, his favorite fallback response was: "Because I say so…."

As time went on, I kept dreaming up more interesting questions about how things worked and why things were the way they were—and not some other way. And the harder the questions got, the more I heard "just because." One time I complained to mom her "just because" response was an *unsatisfactory* answer.

I made sure she was *out of earshot* before I said this, of course.

Finally, as an act of self-defense, they eventually splurged and bought a brand-new set of *World Book* Encyclopedias from our family's meager budget.

What an *amazing* gift to the family—I loved it. I enjoyed thumbing through its gold-edged pages, and studying its full-color images. I was extra-careful as I studied the fold-out transparencies of frog guts.

The *World Book* was for us *the* source of information on anything and everything. And it was way better than the cheapo encyclopedias that we'd been collecting down at Safeway. We had a partial set of those plasticized books that came free if you bought enough groceries, but they paled in comparison to our new acquisition. The *World Book* was elegantly bound, and made to last a lifetime.

Better still, it grew two inches each January as the yearbooks documented the steady advances of mankind.

The books took up so much space that my folks bought a new, ornate and sturdy bookcase to house them all. The golden-trimmed set gleamed in the light, looking like a shrine to all things intellectual.

My parents' purchase paid off almost immediately.

Now when I bugged them with questions, Mom had a new response.

"You should look it up," she'd say, and point with all the accuracy of a compass towards the *World Book*.

And I did.

I looked up anything and everything. Some days I'd just sit and read when we didn't have time to drive down to the library, since it was too far for me, a mere second-grader, to ride my bike all on my own. Mom started calling me "The Encyclopedia Kid." I like that better than the one Dad gave me, "Jughead." I looked that up, and didn't find anything bad. But I didn't like the way it sounded.

As it turned out, mom and dad just traded one set of problems for another. Instead of asking incessant questions, I now wanted to assault everyone with over-the-top answers.

My new MO was to latch onto a friend or family member and rattle off everything I knew about some obscure bit of trivia. For example, I could explain why a glassful of water cracked and busted when my little brother put it in the freezer instead of the fridge. I was so pleased to tell everyone. Strangely, though, Mom and Dad didn't seem equally delighted to learn the science behind this mishap. They were more concerned that there was glass all over the floor and that they no longer had a full set of complimentary Sears water tumblers. And they were too busy punishing my brother to listen to me.

Where was their appreciation of science?

It got to the point my family would run when they saw me coming, and so I turned my attention to school.

I *loved* being in school. I couldn't wait until the teacher would ask a question. I mean this quite literally, I'd just start talking whenever it suited me. When the teacher *did* ask a question, I'd shoot my hand up, and whether I was called on or not, launch into a five-minute, encyclopedically detailed answer.

I viewed these moments as the sort of Q&A game shows, like Password or the Quiz Kids. I was determined to be the final, holdout contestant. I figured the *World Book* had equipped me to answer just about *any* question. I had so much excess intellectual energy and information that I was eager to answer questions, even ones that weren't even being asked!

One day during 2nd grade math, I was sitting next to Randy and explaining why life could exist on Earth but not on many of the other planets in the solar system. *Hint: It's mostly about the size of our planet and its distance from the sun.*

I'd just finished sharing this when I was suddenly dragged out of my seat and hauled up to the front of the classroom. I looked around, a bit disoriented, and saw the same half-finished subtraction problem that had been on the board for *ages*.

For a moment, I thought that maybe Mrs. Reyes had overheard me and wanted me to share my fun science facts with the class.

Apparently not—without saying a word, Mrs. Reyes scribbled a few sentences on a referral slip and sent me packing to the principal's office. Once I arrived, it didn't take long for Mr. Lewis to get to the point.

"Mrs. Reyes says you were disrupting the class with chatter," he said.

"I was helping Randy," I said. "I wasn't interrupting."

"Really?" He held up the note. "Mrs. Reyes says the entire back row was listening to you talk about science fiction."

"No sir," I said.

"So Mrs. Reyes is making things up?"

"I was telling him why there's no life on the Moon."

"I'm sure that's interesting," he said, "but Mrs. Reyes says she was in the middle of a subtraction problem. You need to learn subtraction."

"Yes, sir, but science uses subtraction, too."

Mr. Lewis sighed.

"Perhaps, but you were not paying attention," he said.

"But I already *knew* the answer," I said, "and so did Randy."

"Well, not everyone does, and they were trying to learn," he said.

"But you said they were listening to me." I reminded him.

His face turned red.

"The point is that they were working out a *math* problem and *you* need to be polite to your teacher."

"But she took forever explaining an *easy* problem, and I could tell Randy needed help," I said. "Then we just used our extra time to talk about science."

"Science is good," Mr. Lewis said. "But Randy needs to listen to Mrs. Reyes, and *you* must stay focused and watch your teacher at *all* times."

I mulled over Mr. Lewis' "staying focused" advice for a moment, and it seemed a pretty dull way to go through life. There are *so many* interesting things happening, often at the same time. I mean, why stick with just one flavor of ice cream when you can get Neapolitan? Even when I'm reading the *World Book*, my favorite part of the article is at the end when it tells you to *see also*. These two magic words will send you to a different topic and another adventure. There is just *no telling* what you'll find, and it shows you that everything in the world is so *connected*.

So, jumping around from one thing to the next seems like a *great* idea to me.

I was reflecting on all this while Mr. Lewis waited, drumming his fingers. Finally, he thumped a fist on his desk and interrupted my thoughts.

"So, Robb, I do *not* want you bothering your classmates and bringing up other topics while Mrs. Reyes is teaching."

"Why not?"

Mr. Lewis looked at me through narrow eyes.

"Talking in class is against the *rules*."

"But can we *change* the rules?" I asked.

"No, *we* can't." Mr. Lewis shook his head.

I sat, lost in thought. Surely there had to be a solution to this problem.

"Maybe I could talk to rule person," I said helpfully.

"You *are* talking to the rule person,"

"Oh," I said, a bit confused. "Then maybe *you* could change the rule?"

"No. That's not going to happen."

"How come?" I asked.

"Because it's a good rule," he said, crossing his arms.

"Oh," I replied and looked at him intently, waiting for a further explanation. But none came. After a few moments, I realized this was a non-verbal *"Because I say so."* I knew the conversation was over when he turned away from me and began writing a hall pass.

Note to the World Book people: You should add an article on this silent-treatment tactic; it's one of those tricks adults use to win arguments. My mom could write it for you.

So Mr. Lewis made me promise that I wouldn't talk or act up again. I did, and he wrote a note for Mrs. Reyes and I returned to class

I kept this promise for all of 15 minutes or so, and then, without thinking, I began to explain to a classmate where water goes when it disappears from a cup sitting in the sun.

I spent the rest of the afternoon waiting in the office, staring at a wall.

***

Later that day, Mom had to stop by the principal's office to pick me up. When she arrived, Mr. Lewis pulled her into his office and they had a little chat. She emerged a few minutes later shaking her head.

Mom took my hand, and we headed home.

"You were talking in class … again?" she asked.

I nodded.

"You know it makes Mrs. Reyes angry."

"Yeah," I said.

"So why did you do it?" Mom asked. "Mr. Lewis doesn't know what to do with you!"

I stopped to think, but for once I didn't have a ready answer.

I shrugged.

"How come?" Mom persisted.

"Because …." I said, trying to dream up something that she'd find acceptable.

Mom stopped and looked me in the eye.

"Because of *what?*" she asked.

I stood there, chewing my lip.

After a tense moment, Mom sighed. "Honestly, son, why *do* you do this?"

I was sad—I knew I'd disappointed her. But since my genius-ideas hadn't impressed Mr. Lewis, I decided to play it safe and use the answer I'd heard most often at home— from *her*.

"Well, Mom, because … just because," I said.

"And that's *it?*" Mom asked.

I shrugged and then nodded.

"Because … just because," she repeated, and then after a moment, laughed.

"Now there's the *perfect* answer," Mom said, and winked. "And be sure to use it the next time Mr. Lewis asks you a question."

Then she hugged me, gave me a thumbs up sign, and let the subject drop.

So in the end, I conceded Mom's point. There are times the only acceptable explanation is still, just *because*.

fifteen

SNAZZING IT UP WITH SCIENCE

Fifth period with Mr. Paul was my *favorite* time of day. An instant after taking our seats, the show would begin.

"Who knows the difference between hydrogen and helium?" Mr. Paul asked. He tapped a rubber-tipped pointer, the length of a walking stick, on a chart tacked to the wall. He moved the pointer between a blue box that contained the number "1" and the letter "H" and a yellow box with a "2" and the letters "He." The boxes sat atop many other boxes that made the chart look like a city skyline.

"Is he *kidding?*" I whispered to my friend Chris. No teacher in his right mind would ask a from-the-book question on the first day of school, especially right after lunch.

Mr. Paul smiled, arched his eyebrows, and looked out on his class. Half the students were fidgeting in fear of being called on, the other half daydreamed and looked out the big bank of windows to the left of the room.

"Any thoughts from the front row?" Mr. Paul fixed his gaze on Chris.

Chris slowly raised his hand. "They're both gasses."

Mr. Paul smiled broadly, and nodded. "Right you are, Mr. Olson. But what are their unique characteristics?"

Silence. Mr. Paul puckered his lips up, like he was going to whistle. But instead he reached over and picked up a yellow balloon clipped to a metal stand. He released the clip, drew the balloon to his face, and inhaled deeply. The balloon shrank a bit.

"Would a demonstration help?" The question came from Mr. Paul's mouth, but it was in a chipmunk-voice.

The class erupted in laughter.

"Does this give you a clue?" Mr. Paul tied a string to the balloon, and released it. It floated lazily to the ceiling.

"That's helium," Chris said, pointing towards the yellow balloon on the ceiling. "My Dad did that at my sister's party."

"Maybe. But how do you know that it's helium and not hydrogen? Both are light gasses." As he spoke, Mr. Paul picked up another metal stand, this one with a red balloon. It had a string on it, and Mr. Paul let it drift towards to the ceiling near the other balloon.

"Well, Dad said that they use helium," Chris said.

"You're right. But...." he paused and looked up and across row after row of rapt faces. "Do you know why?" Mr. Paul pointed at the two balloons. "One of these balloons contains helium, the other hydrogen." He reeled them both in, and tied them to the metal stand. "As you correctly note, helium is widely used for party balloons." He thumped both balloons.

"But both float rather nicely, don't you think?" The class nodded. "So, why use one instead of the other?"

"Maybe helium's cheaper?" Chris said.

"No, it's not." Mr. Paul winked. "But good guess. Any other thoughts?"

More silence, as 28 minds turned the question over.

"Let's do a little experiment, and you tell me which balloon has helium, and which has hydrogen." Mr. Paul lit a Bunsen burner attached to a long rubber tube, and he then used the pointer to maneuver the yellow balloon over to the flame.

The classroom began to smell of charred rubber, and then the balloon imploded with a muffled snort that almost put the flame out. Mr. Paul used the pointer to flick the smoldering balloon into the sink. "Interesting, no?"

Chris and I exchanged startled looks. This was the first time I ever saw an adult burn something on purpose that wasn't in a fireplace or an incinerator.

Next, Mr. Paul slid the burner over to the red balloon.

BANG! The balloon disappeared in a cloud of flame that rushed up towards the ceiling, and 28 bottoms simultaneously jumped up from their seats. The fireball vanished as suddenly as it appeared, and smoldering bits of rubber lay all about the table.

Pandemonium broke out—laughing, shouting, and chattering like none of us had ever heard in class when the teacher was present.

Mr. Paul had not flinched or changed expression once during the experiment, and now he stood with an innocent smile on his face, waiting for the noise to subside on its own accord. At length, it did.

"So, class, which balloon had the hydrogen? And, for extra credit, why don't we use hydrogen balloons at birthday parties?"

Dozens of hands shot up demanding attention.

It was in that instant that we fell in love with Mr. Paul and took our first steps forward as scientists. For us, it was the end of daydreaming in class and wishing we were somewhere else. The fire that he lit in us on day one has burned ever since and remains as one of my most vivid memories.

sixteen

BEING KNOTTY

My kid brother and I had fussed for years for a tree house. We'd asked Dad. We'd asked Santa. We'd even gone to church to ask God. Nothing seemed to work.

For the longest time, we just pretended we had a tree house. Anytime our neighbors bought an appliance, we'd confiscate the box, cut windows in it, and haul it up into the old mulberry in the back yard. This was not really a good idea because, if you weren't careful, you could take a step and either go through the floor or tumble off a branch, box and all, to the bushes below. Not only that, but we were forced to sit closer to one another than brothers are supposed to sit. We often fought over the box, and the fastest climber got first dibs. The loser could either wait, or try to force the winner out by pelting him with golf balls and rocks.

Usually the loser in these battles was the box. If the rocks didn't kill the box, then the struggle to be the first one in would often rip the box and send us both into the bushes. One afternoon I managed to knock my brother Jim out of the tree three times. I thought this was an amazing accomplishment in the annals of tree warfare, but my mother took a dim view of my victory. Each time Jim fell out, he got a bloody nose and had to go into the house to change his shirt. He'd run through his entire wardrobe by the time Mom told us that "enough is enough."

We were grounded, and reduced to watching television. This lasted for all of one day, in which time we broke the remote control and then ruined my sister's new canopy bed when we tried to use it as an indoor tree house.

So it was that we came home from school the next day to see a wonder, a two-level tree house complete with railing, real windows, and a rope ladder that could be drawn up in case of enemy attack. We were stunned. It wasn't Christmas, or anyone's birthday. We hadn't been to church in a few weeks, and no one had gotten a good report card. Why this had finally happened, after all these years, was a mystery to us.

But there it was. We rubbed our eyes and it didn't go away. My dad had taken a rare day off of work, and gone to the lumber yard and bought new lumber, still green and sticky, to build a tree house, *our* tree house.

Before we could take possession, Mom sat Jim and me both down and told us her *one rule* of the tree house—there was to be no more fighting. Period. It was both of ours. We had to share and share alike. Jim and I scowled at each other. I figured it would be mine, because I was bigger and older, and Jim figured it would be his when I wasn't around, which was often. But worse news soon followed. Even our little sister could come up if she wanted to. She was too little to climb the ladder now, but when the day came that she could, then it would be hers too.

What a rip-off! We'd waited for years for our tree house, and our bratty little sister was going to get one before she was even old enough to know how special it was. After all, tree houses are sacred, secret places where adults are not allowed, and we were going to have to let a *girl* come up there? Our sister, no less!

Jim and I sat, deflated, as she laid down the law.

"The only reason we build this tree house is to stop all the fighting around here," Mom said. "It will give you a place to go, to burn off some energy, and there's room enough for all of you up there. That's why we made it so big." She paused and looked at us both. Pat was in the other room, playing with Muffy, her three-foot-tall, life-sized doll. She was not at all interested in the negotiations that were giving her a share in our prime real estate.

Mom looked at us, slumped in our chairs, and frowned. "You two don't seem at all grateful. Your father worked all day on this, and we spent the money we were going to use to go to the beach next month. So, I'd expect a bit more gratitude and a lot less attitude."

"Yes Mom," Jim and I said, kowtowing in perfect unison.

"And be sure to thank your father when he gets home."

"Yes Mom."

"Well, aren't you going to try it out?" She smiled, cocked her head and let her gaze roll over us and out to the back yard. We turned away from her and looked again at the tree house, *our* tree house. Jim and I quickly nodded at one another, knowingly—we'd discovered that it's one thing to make a rule, quite another to make it stick.

So we howled and hooted, scrambled out the door, ran shoulder to shoulder all the way. I managed to grab the rope before Jim and scampered up with him pulling at my shoes. He just missed getting a bloody nose.

We both climbed to the upper deck, and looked out upon our neighborhood, from our new command post. Maybe there was room enough for both of us up here, and maybe we'd invite our friends, too. If you're going to have a fort, then you need some troops to man the garrison. From this new height, we looked about carefully for potential threats and opportunities for adventure.

***

I don't remember if it was Jim or I who first noticed the extra coil of rope that my dad had so thoughtfully left for us in the tree house. What a wise man our father was. We'd need this to haul up all manner of supplies and tools to equip our fortress. This we did with gusto, bringing up our treasures: wobbly chairs scrounged from neighbors' garages, castoff sleeping bags with broken zippers, golf balls and other projectiles, and my dad's binoculars.

Beyond this, Jim and I disagreed on what belonged in the fort. He was all for the WW II look, and my mind was still aflame in the age of Hollywood Westerns. I wanted bows and arrows, a Winchester Rifle, a red-hot branding iron, and a Bowie knife, but these were not easy to come by with pacifist parents. We agreed to split our fort, I took the upper level, complete with the trap door. This settled, we each went for our own ideal of tree-fort décor; Jim wasted no time in hauling up his entire GI Joe collection. Apparently my parents didn't mind warfare if it came in miniature boxed sets. But I was out of luck. I couldn't even get my hands on a cowboy hat.

I suffered terribly.

One day, as I sat wearing my outlaw's bandanna, I looked at my side. There was just an open, empty space. I wracked my brain to think of where I could come up with a pistol. Maybe I should invite some friends over and play with *their* cap-guns. I was thinking of how we could smuggle all this contraband past my Mom, when I noticed the rope. It was lying there in a heap, filthy and ratty looking. I picked it up, and wound it around my forearm as I'd seen my father do so many times before.

I felt the coarseness of the hemp, and rolled it back and forth in my hands, and I watched the end spin in wobbly circles. It was hypnotizing, and as I studied this rope a primitive joy and epiphany seized me.

I had *rope*.

The two things that *really* make a cowboy a cowboy, rope and Levis. Cowboys could lose their weapons, and still be cowboys, so long as they had *rope*. It was true that all the guys I knew wore blue jeans, but how many had rope?

No one but *me!*

I was overjoyed, and to think that I'd missed this. What a dope I'd been. It was like I'd been tripping over a bar of gold each day and then complaining that the stupid brick just kept getting in my way.

But rope was *better* than gold.

My brother could have his little plastic men. Rope was real, and ripe with possibilities.

I tied the end into a loop and began lassoing all the objects in the fort. The chair with its wobbly wheels gave me a little fight coming over to my side. Our chest full of blankets was harder to lasso and drag. Beyond that… what else could I catch?

Below me there was our cat, Tommy. He was watching, hoping to snag my sandwich leftovers. I rolled the rope between my fingers, judging the distance. But he was a bit out of range. He licked his lips, anticipating a tasty meal. But then he must have read my mind because he turned and bolted to safety.

Rats. I had to look for other prey.

Near the base of our tree sat my sister's tricycle. It was an easy target. I flicked my snare and hit it on the first try. Then I hauled it up into the fort. Not many cowboys ride a trike but, hey, I was in outlaw mode. And rustling is rustling. You take what you can grab and still make a clean getaway. I'd done that, but what now? I surveyed the yard and could see nothing more to snag.

Sure, I tried lassoing birds that roosted here in the branches, but it was mostly to pass the time and to work on my aim. I had nothing to show for my troubles except a pile of leaves.

Events might have gone on like this forever if Chris

hadn't dropped by. Chris was my smartest friend, an only child and the son of a librarian. He was full of great ideas. When he looked at my rope, he immediately knew what to do.

"You need to make a hangman's noose."

"Exactly!" I shouted with joy. "But how?" We'd both seen hangman's nooses in action, but we'd never seen one tied.

Who to ask? This wasn't a knot I'd ever seen in Dad's old Boy Scout manual left over from my grandparent's aborted attempt at applied civics. No one I knew had ever shown me how to tie such a knot.

"It's got to be written down somewhere," Chris ventured. "Mom says that everything you'd ever want to know is in a book. You just have to know where to look." So, we dug into our Hardy Boy books, but they skirted all the useful skills a boy really needed. Zane Grey failed us, and the World Book had nothing useful to add on the subject either. We looked under "Knots," "Cowboys," and "Cattle-rustling."

Our faith in the printed word was shaken, but we had one last trick—visit the library. We pedaled down to the Oildale library and put our research question to the grim woman with the gray bun. Shortly thereafter, Chris and I were escorted off the premises by the janitor.

***

Our quest wasn't going well at all, until we met Sam Young outside the 7-11. He was there pretending to be the world's oldest and largest Cub Scout, mooching bottles for change. He'd just panhandled enough for a large Slurpee.

Chris and I explained our problem as Sam downed his drink.

"You won't believe this, but the library doesn't have a single book on hangman's knots."

Sam laughed so hard he snorted, and then shook his

head. "You dopes, it's easy." He made Chris remove his shoelace, and stretched it out, zigzagged one end into a flat "S," and wound 13 turns around it, leaving a small loop that he closed with a jerk.

"Here, girls," he said, and tossed us the tiny noose.

In that moment I learned that there's literature, and then there's life. No one could say when Sam last picked up a book, but you had to admit he was the man with the answers. We thanked him, grabbed our little blueprint of death, and raced back to the tree house, Chris' unlaced shoe flapping all the way.

We'd both seen Sam tie the knot, but we weren't sure that we could do it ourselves. So we carefully unwrapped it, and made notes on binder paper, drawing pictures of the knot in various stages of disassembly.

Now it was time to put our knowledge into action, and so we tied our first noose. It looked like a noose, anyway, but it had only 10 turns.

"Gotta have 13 turns," Chris said. "Do it again."

So, I tried again, but it was hard to keep the turns from sliding off the end of the double-slip knot. I'd never seen a real cowboy have this much trouble, but none of them had Chris laughing at them each time they tried.

"Let me do it," Chris said, grabbing at rope.

I pulled it away from him. "Right. Like you could do any better."

The extra rush gave me the push I needed, and I succeeded at last. We had a tightly wound cord with 13 coils supporting a perfect, oval noose. It was a beauty, just waiting to see some action. We hauled the empty noose up, and let it dangle. John Wayne could not have done any better. Now all we needed to do was nab a cattle rustler and give 'em a short trial that would end with a long rope.

Honestly, there had never been any question as to who we were going to hang, once we had "the knot." Muffy was my prime target. Sure, I'd considered other options, but Chris didn't volunteer his services, and my brother would just make too much noise and get us caught, as always. No, the doll was just the ticket. It was the spitting image of her owner, Pat.

It was no problem to lift Muffy from my sister's room while she was taking her afternoon nap.

Chris and I knew that the doll would be missed as soon as Pat woke up, so we had to do our deed quickly and return Muffy before she was missed. There was a brief argument as to who got to be the hangman and who would film the event with Dad's Super-8 movie camera. Chris wanted to do a coin toss, and I argued that it was my rope.

We finally decided that we'd just take turns. It wouldn't take all that long to try and convict Muffy, and then give her a double-dose of frontier justice. I got to go first.

We stood Muffy, blindfolded, on the trap door, and then, after finding her guilty of rustling cattle, robbing a bank, and cheating at checkers, we decreed death by hanging. I pulled the lever, and... nothing. The trap door didn't budge. I tugged again, still nothing. Chris kept the camera rolling, and motioned for me to stomp on the trap door. I shook my head, and motioned for him to stomp on the door. He shook his head. So, I braced myself and yelled "Prepare to meet your maker!" I pushed hard with my right foot, intending to jump clear as the door fell open.

Now, the problem is this. When you are way up there, where you can see everything, then everything and everybody can see you, too. Chris and I were too busy to notice my next-door neighbor, Mrs. K, a cranky, curious, 800-year-old woman, with a weak heart and strong binoculars. She'd been watching us all morning. She spied on us as we tied the noose. She studied us as we dropped and dangled that noose, and Mrs. "K" had her phone in hand as the trapdoor gave way and Muffy and I fell.

What happened next was later pieced together by eyewitness accounts, including those from people who weren't even there. Which story you choose to believe depends on whether you trust your average 11-year-old, disappointed parents, or police reports phoned in by hysterical old ladies.

The simple truth is this:

The doll fell out of the tree.

I tried to grab it.

I managed to avoid serious injury.

The same cannot be said for the doll.

Chris claims that I killed Muffy when I broke my fall by clutching her leg.

Police forensics, aided by the confiscated footage, described the doll's demise as "failure of internal elasticity."

The paramedics who revived Mrs. K said that she seemed incoherent, babbling about "those horrible boys!" and how "they've ripped off the little girl's head!"

My feeling about all this is that, if you're going to be a snoop, you'd better do a good job. After all, Chris and I had just about gathered the pieces when Mom interrupted us with all that screaming. If you stop to think about it, it's really the police dispatcher's fault for scaring her like that.

So, I lost my tree house privileges for a month, and I've been banned from using rope until I'm 216 years old.

Chris says that Mrs. K should have been busted for filing a false report, but she wasn't. Life just isn't fair. Where's frontier justice when you need it?

seventeen

THE PURLOINED PLAYBOY

Chris pulled a tattered magazine from behind his bed's headboard and waved it at me.

"Check this out," he said.

The cover featured a blonde curled up on a bed, pillow wedged behind her, legs carefully folded in such a way that she might, or might *not*, be wearing underwear.

I pretended not to notice the picture, and read the caption next to it. "So, who are the 'Girls of Russia'?"

Chris looked at me with amazement. "Hello? How about the babe?"

"Oh, yeah," I said awkwardly. "She looks kinda angry."

"You're weird," Chris said, and sat the Playboy down on his bed. He lightly touched the cover, poking Olga on her red headband, and Chris then worked his way slowly, page-at-a-time, towards Miss March.

"Wow," I said finally. "How'd you get this?"

"It wasn't easy," Chris said, "I had to pay Gary fifty cents and pinky swear a secret."

"What secret?"

Chris looked at me with annoyance. "Hello! It's a

secret." But then he returned his attention to the magazine. Even the ads were exotic. The articles, on Lenny Bruce and Shel Silverstein, were probably interesting, too, but it would be years before we'd claim to have read them.

"Why did Gary sell it?" I asked.

Chris smiled wickedly. "That's the pinky-swear secret."

Obviously, Chris had the goods on Gary. It must have been an interesting bit of extortion. Gary was the one classmate we had who could pound *any* of us, so you didn't want to cross him. But Gary's dad owned a long-haul trucking outfit, and he had access to the drivers' lounge and all its treasures—including stacks and stacks of men's girly magazines. According to Gary, he swiped the duplicate copies and no one seemed to miss them.

It boggled my mind to think that there was a place that would have copies of Playboy just lying around. It must have been one of the company's fringe benefits.

I stared at the magazine while Chris leafed through it. He didn't offer to let me *touch* the magazine, but I didn't need to. I could feel the heat coming off of it even as I sat next to him on his bed.

Chris reached the centerfold, and opened it up like an art curator might take the protective wrappings off the Mona Lisa, except that this lady had more of a smile and far less in the way of clothing.

While we were oogling the image, and turning it this way and that, a piece of paper fluttered from between the pages.

Chris grabbed it before it hit the ground.

"Look! It's a *subscription* form," he said. His eyes bugged out of his head.

"Imagine what it must be like to get a *new one* each month!"

Chris lapsed into silence, letting his hand slide slowly down Miss March's leg before setting the magazine down in front of him. We stared for a long, long time.

"If you could get a subscription," I said. "Then we

wouldn't have to deal with Gary."

Chris nodded.

"And they print a new one *each* month?" I asked.

"Yeah."

"Wow. I wonder what guys do with the old ones," I said. "Do they throw 'em away?"

Chris slowly shook his head, caressing the image. "Naw. Would *you* throw this away?"

I didn't answer, but I imagined vast storehouses full of Playboys. I looked at the magazine, and saw that the date was 1964. It had been around a while.

"How far back do they go?"

"Back?"

"You know, when did they start?"

"Oh," Chris said, "I think my dad has one from 1953."

"Your *dad* has a Playboy?" I pictured his bespectacled, gray-haired farther with a girlie mag.

"Yeah, a 'collectable.' It has Marilyn Monroe on the cover."

"Who's that?"

"Some hot dead chick."

"That's sick."

"She wasn't dead in the picture," Chris said.

"Yeah, sure."

"No really, it wasn't like that."

We let the topic drop, preferring instead to go through the magazine, now, from back to front.

"Check this out," Chris said, pointing at some fine print. "You can subscribe and get home delivery."

"No way," I said. "They'll bring this right to you?"

"Your mailbox, stupid. You can get it mailed to you."

We both looked at one another, and I wondered if he was thinking what I was thinking.

"Can you come up with $4?" Chris asked.

"But it doesn't cost that much to subscribe." I pointed to the subscription information.

"Yeah, but we'll need a money order, and we'll have to

mail it."

"OK."

"Ought to take about $4 each."

"But who's gonna get it?" I asked. "My mom would kill me."

"Same here. But I've got it figured out."

"Yeah?"

"You know Mr. Morrison?"

"Who?"

"The guy who lives in my folk's rental in back?"

"Yeah?"

"I take him his mail each day."

"So?"

"So, we just use his address, and I grab it before he gets it."

The plan seemed to make perfect sense to me. It did take a couple of weeks to round up that much money. I had to save my allowance and haul a wagon load of bottles to the store. I even had to part with some of my favorite comic books. But in the end, I had my share. Chris bought the money order, and we mailed out the subscription, in the name of T.A. Morrison, to Hugh Hefner Enterprises.

We checked the mail daily, and after what seemed like ages, we saw a bundle, wrapped in brown paper, appear in Mr. Morrison's mailbox. It was like a little bit of heaven had come to Worthington Street.

"So, who gets to keep them?" I asked Chris. This detail had not been worked out, and I saw an immediate problem in our partnership.

"We both own them," Chris said. "But it's easier to keep them here."

"Says you!"

"You think you can keep this, and not get caught?"

Chris had me there. I couldn't get away with anything. Chris could sneak a dead skunk past his mother.

"That's not fair," I mumbled.

"We can talk about it later, OK?" Chris broke open the

wrapper, and we methodically worked our way cover to cover, and back. Between those covers we got the sort of education you just don't get in most public schools.

Chris and I had been close friends for many years, but we now had a deep, common interest and joint investment, one that needed to be guarded as it grew. As with most valuable objects, security is an ongoing concern. Chris had to devise a new hiding place. He opted for the hidden-in-plain-sight approach by pulling the covers off of old National Geographics and then slipping the Playboys into them.

In addition to our monthly subscriptions, Chris managed to fill out his back issues by striking deals with Sam.

"I got this one for a quarter," Chris said, showing me a June issue. "It's missing the centerfold.'

"Ohhh... rats," I said.

"Yeah, I know. But it's better than nothing."

After months of hard work, our collection spanned two full shelves, and Chris and I enjoyed hours of adolescent research into the female form.

There's an old saying that all good things must come to an end, and I learned the meaning of this when Chris and I walked home from school and stopped by his house to find his mother in a flurry of activity.

"What's up?"

"Oh, Chrissy," his Mom said. "Can you be a dear and carry the boxes to the curb?"

We both looked in horror as we saw that she had emptied the shelves of all the magazines and journals.

"Mom?"

"Oh, please hurry. Mr. Turner will be by in a minute. He didn't have room for it all, so he's making one last run, gathering things for the church rummage sale."

Chris looked at me in horror, and I could see that all the shelves that had contained our treasures were empty. Mrs. Olson, with her thick eyeglasses, had not looked closely at the magazines she'd boxed up. And all of that prime material was now on its way to help raise money for St. Benedict's.

"Do we tell her?" I whispered.

Chris shook his head, and we both gathered up a few remaining boxes of Life and Look magazines, lugging them out to the mailbox.

We had one last, desperate, idea. We'd go to the rummage sale and buy them all back. We awoke early that Saturday, skipping all our usual TV shows and pleasures, and pedaled furiously down to Chris' church. We found the sale already in full swing. It's hard to get a jump on the geriatric set.

Chris raced down the aisles, and found the magazine section.

"Here." He motioned me over.

We looked and looked and looked.

"Found anything?" Chris asked.

"Nothing."

Chris worked up the courage to ask one of the church ladies.

"Is this all the magazines?"

"Oh, Christopher. I believe it is."

"Really?"

"Well, I do think they may have sent some of them off to our missionaries."

"Oh," Chris said, a pained, forlorn look on his face.

"But it's all for a good cause," the church lady said. "Part of our larger mission, you know."

So, our treasures were gone. Call it fate, or perhaps the will of the almighty. We learned that day that God really does work in mysterious ways.

And our belief was deepened when, later that week, we learned that Mr. Morrison decided to die, and his estate had all his mail forwarded to his relative in Lithuania.

Chris was crushed, but I comforted him.

"It's all for a good cause," I reminded him.

"Yeah, part of a larger mission," he said.

eighteen

THE ART OF CHEWING GUM

I don't remember my first stick of gum, but I do remember the first time I had gum cut out of my hair. I was four, and had gone to sleep with a wad of double-bubble tucked under my tongue. Of course I'd been told to spit it out before I went to bed. The problem is that I didn't go to bed. Actually, I fell asleep in my Radio Flyer wagon, wrapped in a flannel blanket. Mom scooped me up, didn't think to do a routine sweep of the mouth, and tucked me in.

Gum, I learned, is not inanimate. It crawls, amoeba-like, from your mouth to the location where it can do the most damage. In this case it crawled up my face, across the bridge of my nose, and spread itself out on the hair that covered my forehead. It then permanently bonded with the hair. Sure, Mom tried using ice, like I was a piece of furniture. That didn't work. Dad was all for using gasoline—his answer for all cleaning problems. But after the incident in the laundry room with our water heater, Mom said "no."

"I guess there's only one thing to do," Dad said,

holding my chin in his hand just a tad too tightly. He was mad at me, a bit. But Mom blamed herself. Without letting go, Dad reached for the electric clippers, the same ones that he used on Freckles, our dog.

"Won't he get fleas?" Mom asked.

"Maybe," Dad answered nonchalantly.

"Well, then…"

"If he does," Dad said as he fired up the clippers. "Then we'll try 'Mystery Oil.'" My dad believed that everything in the world could be fixed with either Marvel Mystery Oil or bailing wire. This gum in the hair didn't seem like a bailing wire kind of problem. Not yet anyway.

So I got my first buzz cut. I don't remember much about it, but the pictures provide all the evidence I care to have. Mom saved some of the hair clippings, including ones with the gum. But the pages of the baby book stuck together, and it had to be cut out of there, too.

Gum is really amazing stuff, I decided early on. I became an enthusiastic supporter of Bazooka bubble gum. Chris was an ardent supporter of cinnamon gum. He wanted something with more kick. We occasionally traded gum, and I enjoyed the occasional change, but remained unconverted to Chris' view.

My other buddy, Sam, developed a taste for the horrible stuff that came with baseball trading cards. He got all he wanted from his dad's 7-11. So he was Mr. Generosity in giving the stuff away. But he had few takers. I traded gum with Sam a few times, and decided his gum was only slightly better than chewing the cards that it came with. In fact, sometimes the cards stuck to the gum and when you were chewing you *were* getting a taste of Mickey Mantle or Don Drysdale, a sort of major-league cannibalism that made me briefly lose my appetite for baseball.

But there were things even worse than Sam's stuff—the war-surplus gumballs from the machine down at Miller's Variety. They were cheap, only a penny a piece, and old man Miller must have had a warehouse full of them. But after nearly breaking a tooth, I decided that I'd rather do without.

Other friends specialized in Wrigley's. Mike's mom was a dental assistant, and she made him chew Trident. We felt sorry for him, but not enough that we'd trade with him. Poor Mike was reduced to chewing the baseball-card stuff.

Gum was one of the original wonders in my life. It provided my first lessons in bartering and trading. It also gave me some exercise, relaxation, and various forms of competition.

Chris claimed to hold the record for the longest uninterrupted chewing of a single piece of gum. According to him, he mashed on it all summer between 3rd and 4th grade. We had to take his word for it. But he had the advantage of being the only kid in our class with braces. He would stick the gum in-between the wires when he slept, and resume the next day. The cinnamon, he said, kept it from tasting gross.

Sam, of course, with his access to all the gum in the world, held the record for the largest wad of gum chewed without medical intervention. We'd heard that another kid, over at Standard Elementary, had tried to beat Sam's record but had unhinged his jaw and ended up in the emergency room. After that, the award was retired because no one dared to try again.

As for me, I went after the largest bubble record. This was an ongoing battle between me and Clint, Chris' cousin. Clint kept trying to beat me with his own secret combination of gums from special grocery stores found only near Disneyland. What these gums had in them was known only to Clint and the Food and Drug Administration. But it may explain why Clint disappeared from our lives shortly thereafter. My proudest moment was when I blew a bubble bigger than Mrs. Snelling's beehive hairdo, and I did this with plain old Bazooka. True, it took eight pieces and favorable wind conditions.

But I pulled it off, and I have Chris as my witness. Some victories last for a lifetime.

***

Most of the time, our gum chewing was kept out of the view of watchful adults, and we did just fine. But disaster struck one day at recess

It was late Friday, and I was eager to enjoy a weekend of freedom. But before I could rest, I had serious business to attend to. Clint had challenged me to defend my title, and so he and I were squared off near the swings surrounded by our classmates.

I'd just unwrapped a fresh piece—hoping to expand my lead—when I noticed the enclosed Joe Palooka comic. I stopped chewing to read it, and it made *no* sense. So I reread it another *three* times, and I *still* didn't get the joke. While I was distracted, the yard monitor crept up, grabbed my shirt, and then hauled into Mr. Lewis' office.

***

"So," Mr. Lewis began, inspecting my gum wrapper. "You're chewing gum at school."

"No," I answered truthfully. I'd swallowed the gum in the act of being picked up by the scruff of my neck. This made my answer technically and grammatically correct.

"So, where did this wrapper come from then?"

I pondered this for a moment. "Well, it's hard to say. Safeway or 7-11, most likely."

Mr. Lewis didn't appreciate my attempt at precision. "I mean, didn't this come from a pack of gum?"

Hmmm… This was such an obviously true question that I wondered why he bothered to ask it. Did grownups know so little of gum-chewing that they had to learn from 4th graders?

"Yes, sir," I said finally.

"Well, then. You had been chewing gum?" He fine-tuned his grammar, employing the past-perfect.

"Mr. Lewis, I chew gum all the time," I said.

"You are not supposed to chew gum at school." He pointed his finger at the floor for emphasis. "And just so you'll remember, you can help the janitor clean up this afternoon."

I was then dismissed from the principal's office. He kept my Joe Palooka joke. I figured that maybe he didn't get it either, and needed to ask someone else. But later I learned that it was added to my permanent record.

So, that afternoon, I reported to Mr. Mike's office, a closet full of brooms, mops and cleaning chemicals. He led me to the 6th grade classroom, and there, I was made to get down on my hands and knees, and explore the undersides of the upper-classman's desks.

It was an odd view of a strange new world.

There were mounds and mounds of gum-stalactites. It had never occurred to me that you could store gum in this manner. I'd been trained by Mom to wrap my gum up in the comic it came with. This habit was tied to her top two gum-chewing rules: First, you *always* spit out the gum when you were done and, second, that you *never* toss an unwrapped wad into the garbage or, upon penalty of *death*, upon the ground.

But I didn't always follow her directives.

When I had a good comic, I would save it and swallow my gum. I never told Mom because she was convinced that gum would settle in my guts and swell into massive ball of goo. Then on some random day, I'd suffer a fatal, gum-induced intestinal explosion that would make the evening news. But for the most part, I was a well-behaved gum chewer.

So seeing what the big kids did with their gum was a revelation.

Mr. Mike gave me gloves and some goggles to use, and he told me that I could take breaks, walk around, and get some air as often as I needed. He and Mr. Lewis must have thought I'd be grossed out when I had to scrape gum all afternoon. But I was having a *blast* scraping gum, so the intended lesson didn't exactly stick.

In fact, after I'd accumulated a huge jarful of multi-colored lumps, Mr. Mike told me I could call it quits. But I wanted to keep going, and I asked him if I could keep the scrapings. He turned green and practically shouted "*no!*"

I guess he thought I wanted to eat it. I didn't—I just wanted to look at the stuff under a magnifying glass.

Before I finished, one other super-important thing happened—I learned there is a *secret society* of gum chewers.

This revelation happened when Mr. Mike left the room to clean elsewhere, and a 6th grader named Bruce came in to get his baseball glove. He saw me lying on my back, and laughed.

"Let me guess," Bruce said. "They caught you chewing."

"Yeah," I said absently, focused on the task at hand. I think Bruce thought I was embarrassed, but quite the contrary—I felt like Michelangelo working on the Ceiling of the Sistine Chapel.

"Dummy. Hasn't anyone taught you to chew invisibly?"

Now, I'd heard about the art of the invisible chew. But none of my friends had really managed it. You could always tell when one of us was chewing gum. So, I just looked at him and shrugged.

"Look," Bruce said, peeking over his shoulder to make sure no one was watching. "It's easy. Just do this." He whipped out a stick of Juicy Fruit, tore it into *thirds*, and then popped a piece into this mouth. He carefully re-wrapped the rest in the foil.

"Now what?" I asked.

He smiled and came right up to me.

"Can you tell?" he asked through clenched teeth.

"Tell *what*?"

"Exactly." He smiled triumphantly. "You just slide your jaws up and back, and maybe a bit side to side."

I nodded.

"Never unclench. That's the secret. You can chew all day this way."

"But what if the teacher calls on you?"

"Easy. Pucker your lips like you're thinking hard. Then you slide it over and stick it to the roof of your mouth."

Wow, I thought. The things you learn in sixth grade. Here I was, in a punishment detail, and I discovered what many convicts know. Doing time can be instructive.

I finished up cleaning the desks, and wrote the usual letter of apology—hard to do when you're apologizing for something that 100% of the *entire world* does.

But in return, I'd become a member of the secret society of gum chewers, a group of artists that includes all sixth graders and an unknown quantity of adults.

It was the best gum-trade I ever made.

nineteen

GREAT EXPECTORATIONS

I was hawking up a loogie, my fourth or fifth, and taking aim, when Mr. Silvias strode over and grabbed me. He pulled me away from the line of 7th grade boys, all 18 of us in alphabetical order, and began his interrogation.

Now, I wasn't the first person to spit while we waited outside the auditorium, but I was the one the yard-duty teacher saw near the puddle that had, just moments before, been ordinary, dry asphalt.

"What's this?" Mr. Silvias pointed to the patch of bubbling froth—the combined effort of more than 10 sets of salivary glands working unattended for almost 5 minutes.

My first inclination was to feign invisibility, not of my person but of the puddle. But the spit-pond, as it was later to be called, was not easily ignored. It could easily have consumed several basketballs. So, I looked at our impromptu act of liquid defiance and answered honestly: "A puddle, sir."

"And *how* did it get here?" He bent over to put his face right in mine, and I could see the blood vessels in his eyes and the afternoon stubble of his beard. His breath smelled like licorice.

I looked over at my classmates, especially all the boys that had created this new geographical feature. We'd been waiting in line to see a performance by a man who could play three saxophones, all at once. But we had been left to stand in the sun for what seemed like hours. Mr. Silvias was over talking with Miss Tremble, the new Spanish teacher, and she was apparently more interesting than we were. So, we waited, and waited and waited... bored silly.

Bobby decided to amuse himself by spitting on a beetle. He missed, but Gary spit and hit it. Then, in an instant, the race to liquefy the beetle was on.

But stink beetles are tough, and pretty soon all of us were working on a fruitless attempt at collective homicide. So while Mr. Silvias grilled me, the beetle swam free and was high-tailing it towards the shop building.

My silence may have been protected by the 5th Amendment, but 12-year-olds don't have civil rights – I guess that comes with the Constitution curriculum in 8th grade.

"Well!" Mr. Silvias said even louder.

I stared helplessly at my classmates. A few were looking at me and shaking their heads, the rest had taken a sudden interest in the cloud formations above us. The girls were all giggling.

I opened my mouth; it felt like it was stuffed with cotton. "I think I need a drink of water."

"I'll bet you do," he said, pursing his lips. He then drew himself up to his full height, a towering figure of well over six feet, and adjusted his tie. He pressed his lips into a thin, straight line, and stared at the gaggle of boys all standing next to the offending puddle.

We all stared at our shoelaces.

Then he turned to the girls.

"What do any of you know about this?" One of the girls, Pamela, raised her hand.

"Yes, Pamela?" he said.

"The boys were spitting," she replied.

Mr. Silvias scowled. This rather obvious answer clearly didn't please him, but he nodded understandingly towards the girls, and an instant later whirled to face me and my friends.

"Fine, gentlemen. Then you can remain here while the girls go with Miss Trembly's class."

The boys of Mr. Silvias' 6th period history class never got to see just how it is possible to play more than one saxophone at once. I'm sure it put a dent in our cultural upbringing. But I can tell you how many rolls of paper towels it takes to sop up a small, man-made lake. It takes about 9 rolls, half a roll for each boy. It also takes the knees out of your Levis while you crawl around the parking lot, scrubbing up all the water that the janitor used to hose down our project.

There was the usual note home, explaining the nature of our offense and why our jeans suddenly had a year's worth of wear. Mom wanted to know why I'd decided to participate in the "spittle-fest" as Mr. Silvias described it.

"Ah, Mom. He was just exaggerating."

"Really?" she said, raising an eyebrow.

"You know Mr. Silvias. He's the only teacher in the world who wears a tie to teach."

"So?"

"So, he probably has never had a booger or spit in his life."

Mom rolled her eyes.

"It's only natural for guys to spit once in a while," I added.

"It's 'natural' to go to the bathroom, but you don't do that in public, either," Mom countered.

"Yeah, well, OK. But I don't think Mr. Silvias ever goes to the bathroom either."

Mom laughed. "I doubt that."

"He's just not human."

"Maybe not, but then maybe you have to have something a little bit wrong with you to want to teach 7th grade boys." She winked. "You're not exactly human, yet."

She had me there. I had to promise never to spit in public again, at least until I had graduated 7th grade and was no longer in Mr. Silvias' class. I also had to write the usual letter of apology. But at least Mom didn't tell Dad.

At the time, I was grateful because I thought it would keep me from getting in trouble all over again. But as I got older, I decided it was because he'd have taken my side.

After all, it's only natural to have to spit now and then... especially when stink beetles are around.

twenty

BEE CAREFUL

I dashed across the lawn, barefooted, and Mom yelled to me.

"Be careful," she said, "or you'll get stung."

"Be careful" had to be Mom's #1 bit of advice.

"Be careful, or you'll catch your death of cold."

"Be careful, or you'll burn the house down."

"Be careful, or you'll put your brother in the hospital."

Mom had a pessimistic streak in her. She was convinced that whatever she'd heard about from the Moms' Gossip Network or the Evening News was sure to happen. A disaster lurked in every fun activity or pair of roller skates left in the hallway.

Now, for the record, I never once died, or burned down the entire house. Nothing much had ever happened, if you don't count smoke damage, a few Ace bandages, and a trip to see Doctor Erickson for some splinters that would have come out on their own, eventually. I know this because the doctor said so.

But there was one thing that *did* make me sick, and that was hearing "be careful" a zillion times a day. I had finally found a cure, and it was this: I just ignored Mom's worrying.

***

So, one bright spring morning, I was in the yard skipping across the grass, barefooted, stopping to wiggle my toes in a patch of clover. It was true; the lawn was loaded with bees. They swooped down from our almond blossoms, buzzed around the unmowed dandelions, and then dashed off to enjoy the bottle brush.

Mom was outside, too, repainting our back porch. She watched me in between brushstrokes, and her face was scrunched up with concern.

"Put on your shoes," Mom said.

I feigned a sudden interest in a dandelion, and ignored her.

"I mean it," Mom said in a slightly higher register. "Billy Sullivan stepped on a bee, and his foot swelled up like a watermelon." She stopped for a moment, and waved her brush in the direction of the back door. My sneakers sat there, a pair of socks lying next to them. "Your shoes…"

"Nooo," I wailed.

"Yessss…" she replied. "Right nowwwww!"

"Right Now" was Mom's second favorite command, and it too drove me nuts. I applied the principle of selective attention to that one, too.

I ignored her.

So my next move was to abandon the splendor of the lawn and dash to the driveway. I followed the *intent* but not the letter of her directions. I wasn't going to step on a bee on the concrete—a win for her; but I didn't don my shoes—a win for me.

I thought a draw was a fair deal.

Mom must have agreed—she didn't give chase. Either

that, or because the cement porch between us had a fresh coat of red paint.

My new position by the backside of the garage had two big advantages: It was out of Mom's line-of-sight, and it was smack in the middle of our bottlebrush bushes.

They were humming with bees, with some yellow jackets mixed in for good measure. They found our bottle brush bushes irresistible. In turn, they had a magnetic pull on me.

I watched them crawl in and about the red bristles, wondering what attracted them so. And why didn't they sting each other? The bees and yellow jackets didn't seem to mind, sometimes crawling about on the same blossom.

As I watched, my mind was full of questions. Why didn't yellow jackets make honey? How come they could sting you a bunch of times, but bees only once? Did they all live in the same hive? Were they all the same age? Were bees smarter? Could you teach them tricks? There was no way of knowing without capturing some—in the name of science.

I watched them come, go, fly here and there, crawling all over the red, bristled flowers. There must have been a million of them in the ten foot long row of bushes that separated our front and back yards. I leaned against the garage, letting the wall warm my backside and taking in the sweet smell, my daydreams full of bees. The buzzing was hypnotic, inviting a closer look.

Now, I don't know about your mother, but mine reads minds. While I sized up the scads of bees, forming an action plan, a faint but firm voice came from the porch.

"Leave 'em alooooone," she commanded.

Bummer, I thought. But then I played a hunch. Mom couldn't be sure I was really by the bottlebrush bushes. For all she knew, I'd gone to the playground, just down the street. So, I laid low.

And then, after a moment, she spoke again. "Ron, will you go and see what your son is up to?"

Success! This was not a serious threat. Saturdays, Dad could be found welding. It was hard to tell his abstract art from the wrecked trucks he scavenged to get the metal. But he loved sculpting. Once he was in his garage, nothing short of an earthquake could shake him loose. I could, through the wall, hear his big Lincoln welder revving up as he drew a spark and began to play. He wasn't going anywhere. I should be safe.

So Dad didn't answer Mom, a good sign. He was holed up, and she and the back porch were still covered with paint. As long as I stayed out of sight, the bees and their buddies were all mine.

I just needed a way to capture them. And in a stroke of good fortune, I was next to the one place on the planet—Dad's storage shed—that had everything, if you just dug deep enough.

I tiptoed over to the shed, and found it unlocked. Dad was in the garage with the door closed. So he didn't see me sneak into the shed.

Once inside, I rummaged around for bee-containers. I crawled over a pile of vehicle doors, sideboards, and fenders. They groaned under my weight, but no one came to stop me. I reached Dad's wall of shelves.

He saved *everything*.

I found coils of copper tubing, wire and rope. There were stacks and stacks of coffee cans full of old keys, lead weight, bolts, nails, and screws. And just past the cans, caked in dust, I found what I needed—a stack of screw-top jars. I grabbed one. Surely Dad wouldn't miss it, even though it left a small clean circle on the shelf.

Having the right tool for a job makes all the difference. This jar was perfect. It would allow me to capture the bees and look at them up close. A risk-free, *perfect* solution; Mom would *love* this genius idea.

All the while, the bees had been working, blissfully unaware that a nine-year-old boy was about to pay them a visit. I poked my nose out of the shed, making sure Dad was still in the garage. The roar of the welder told me I was OK. I rolled the jar between my palms. It was still slippery with dust.

Which blossom to choose? After looking them all over carefully. I spied one just about waist-level that was alive with motion. In one smooth movement, I jammed the jar over an insect-covered flower and then slapped the lid down hard.

A great choice! I counted a dozen or more bees, and almost as many yellow jackets. Perfect for my project. Pure joy and elation, and a smug feeling of how Mom had been so wrong. There was nothing to worry about. Except… for just one small problem.

The flower was still attached to a thick, woody stalk.

I worked the lid back and forth, back and forth, trying to cut the branch. No luck.

The bees inside the jar had dropped to the bottom, and were bouncing around. I worried that they might hurt themselves.

But it was then that I noticed that the yellow jackets were making a different move, straight at the gap between the lid and the jar. I watched as the biggest one twisted and turned to extricate itself.

Slowly, its yellow head poked out.

I was trapped like a monkey that had grabbed the banana in a jar and couldn't let go. Sweat burned in my eyes as I frantically worked my little glass trap, trying to contain the humming mass of anger. I shook the jar to move them down. It did knock them free, for a second. Then they redoubled their efforts.

I was absorbed in this task, terror welling up in my heart. I hadn't noticed that Jim had slipped up in front of me. Mom had sent him to spy, no doubt.

Jim stood there with a big grin on his face, taking it all in. He snickered, and I looked up to see him covering his mouth with amusement. My terror turned to anger.

"I'm telling," he chortled.

Yikes! I thought. There's *no way* I'm going to get caught standing here like a dope.

Instinctively, I stepped back and yanked on the bush with all my might. The jar came free as the branch bent, broke and bounced back into place—catapulting a swarm of winged stingers on my brother. If ever a moment deserved the caption "And the tables turned," this would be it.

It was, in a word, satisfying.

I watched my tattletale brother take flight. There seemed to be some justice in this world after all. And I was enjoying the moment right up to the point that one yellow jacket slipped out of the jar and nailed me on the back of my hand.

"Yow!" I tried to stifle a scream. "Ahhhh!" I gasped.

In just an instant, my hand was on fire. It hurt so much, I could barely think. But I did remember Mom's horror stories of swelling, suffering, and death. I could just make out Jim's wailing fading into the distance. He was calling for Mom, and that seemed like a pretty good idea—but I couldn't. I'd never hear the end of it if I ran to her.

Ice! That's what I needed. There was a bag full of it in the garage. But Dad was in there, and I couldn't be seen with a bottle of bees in my possession, given the circumstances. After all, Rule #1 in damage control is to maintain deniability.

So I took aim at the shed—the door stood open—and threw the jar as far as I could. I heard it crash against the back wall just as I stepped, as calmly as I could manage, into the garage.

What luck! Dad was out. I immediately grabbed a handful of ice, and parked myself in a corner. My plan now was to just blend in and wait for the furor to die down. But the heat, and the stings were making me feel woozy ...

Ages later, I woke up with a start, my hand throbbing and my pants all wet from the melted ice. But still no sign of Dad, or anyone. Odd.

I was still feeling pretty crummy, but it was time to sneak back to my bedroom and "act natural." This is a cultivated art, a talent not possessed by all. I was up for the task. I looked pretty normal, except for my puffy hand. I tried not to look too grim or guilty. There was always the chance that my brother just might have forgotten to mention how all those bees took such an interest in him.

The porch was still wet as I tip-toed past it and through the kitchen. I noticed a set of small, red footprints, and I followed them into the front room. I found the rest of my family gathered around the TV, looking spent.

Dad was passed out in his recliner, his head covered with bumps that were smeared with a white ointment. Mom had a broad, red band all the way up her right leg, continuing on to her shirt top. The side of her face had a pinkish tinge, the sort a good scrubbing leaves behind. In all, it gave her the look of one of those hot-rods with a racing stripe. She was bent over my little brother. He'd been wrapped in a blanket, and had an empty Rocky Road container next to him. Jim was the only one in the room with a smile.

I tried to stroll past and reach the sanctity of my bedroom.

"And where do you think you're going?"

Sometimes, the best answer is the truth.

"My bedroom," I said.

"Sit down." Mom turned to face me, pointing at the double-rocker. I sat down.

"So," she looked me over head to toe. "Bee sting?"

"No."

"Really?"

"Yellow jacket," I said.

She sighed. "You knew what I meant."

"But you said…."

"And did you do this to your brother?"

I looked at the swaddled form of Jim. Did Mom think I'd wrapped him in a blanket? And was *that* a problem? He seemed happy as a clam and was the only guy in the room without a sting.

Mom saw my puzzled look, and without a word reached over and held up Jim's shoes spattered with red paint.

"Oh," I said with relief. "I didn't do *that.*"

Mom nodded, but squinted skeptically.

"So, you didn't intentionally throw bees on him?"

Oh *that* that, I thought.

Now, I paused to reflect. I learned in school that you have to listen very carefully to *each and every* word in the question to give a proper answer. I knew the answer Mom was expecting to hear. But then she'd gone and put that word "intentionally" in there.

"No," I said, and wondered if I was about to be pounded or grounded.

"You had nothing to do with this?" Mom said.

Darn, I thought. This is a different question altogether. My moment of truth, maybe?

And then, possibly intoxicated by ice cream and Saturday cartoons, Jim spoke up.

"He didn't, Mama."

This was an *amazing* development—I held my breath.

Mom didn't take her eyes off me. "Is that true?"

Normally, I'd have asked for clarification. What exactly in *this* case, is *that?* Or even more importantly, what is *truth?*

Still, it didn't seem wise to press on the semantics.

Mom put her had on Jim's forehead, no doubt checking for fever-induced delirium. She then strode over to me, grabbed my hand, and dragged me around the corner into the kitchen.

I wasn't sure what was happening. Mom sat me down with a thunk and then took a seat across from me.

"You're his big brother," she said and paused, looking intently at me.

I thought for a moment that maybe she had been

breathing the paint fumes too long. Did I need to be told this?

"Do you know he worships you?" Mom continued.

Now I was pretty sure she must have some sort of fever. She couldn't be talking about my little brother, the snitch.

I just stared at her. I had expected a "talk," but not this.

"And as his big brother, I expect you to look out for him."

She waited, and I waited for her to say something. I was sweating, and trying to decide if it would have been less painful to just get stung again or swatted, and get it all over with. But Mom just kept watching me, like I was the bee inside of a jar.

"Well," Mom said.

"I'm glad he's OK," I said, and it was true. I figured I'd be in a lot more trouble if he'd have gone to the hospital.

"I know you are," Mom said, her face relaxing a bit. "But you have to be *extra* careful when your little brother is around. OK?"

"OK," I said automatically.

"I mean it. He'll follow you into trouble. And then what?"

I hate questions like this. What do you say? And then he'll get in trouble? He'll get me in trouble?

"I don't know." I said.

"Then he'll knock his mother into a can of fresh paint!" she shouted.

I guess I deserved that much.

"Yeah," I said in my smallest voice. "That's what happened?"

Mom threw her hands up, looked skyward, and shouted, "and he doesn't even *know*, God." She continued staring at the ceiling for a few moments with that *why have you done this to me look*, and then returned her gaze to me

She now spoke in a barely audible voice, "I told you to stay away from the bees."

I nodded.

"And then this happens," she waved her arms, first pointing towards the front room, then bee-bushes, and then the porch.

I shifted in my chair and scratched the back of my hand. It looked like I was wearing a catcher's mitt since I quit putting ice on it.

Mom's mouth dropped open, and she grabbed my arm.

"Why didn't you come in right away?"

"I fell asleep in the garage," I said.

She stroked the hand, and rolled it gently between her palms.

I winced.

"Well, this needs to be iced." She stood, and put together an ice pack. She worked in silence for several minutes, and then looked at me with a business-as-usual expression.

"OK," she said. "I want you to sit down with your brother and watch TV."

Hmm, I thought. Not often I'm told to watch TV.

"Just so you know," Mom said. "He didn't tell on you."

"Oh," I said.

"And he was terrified." She looked at me sternly.

"Yeah?"

"That's why he ran right through me, trying to get in the house."

I looked at her, and noticed for the first time how tired she looked. When I was smaller, she used to ask me, "are you part of the problem, or part of the solution?"

Today, I knew that I hadn't been part of the solution.

And for the first time, I said "I'm sorry," and really, really meant it.

"Next time," Mom said, "just be careful." She motioned towards the front room.

I headed out, and then she stopped me.

"One other thing," she said. "You wouldn't know how a jar full of wasps fell off Dad's storage shelf and hit him on the head?"

I pondered the question.

"Wasps?" I said. "I don't know anything about wasps."

"Really," she said.

"Yeah," I said, and scurrying out of the kitchen, adding "only yellow jackets and bees."

twenty one

THERE'S NO SUCH THING AS GHOSTS

Saturday Morning, 6 am.

"There's no such thing as ghosts," Dad said, frowning. He scratched out this sentence on the kitchen chalkboard usually dedicated to grocery lists.

He rubbed his face, the heavy stubble of his beard making a different sort of scratching noise against his calloused hand.

"Say it." He tapped his finger on the board.

Even though I couldn't read his handwriting, I obeyed.

"There's no such thing as ghosts."

"So, the next time you wake your mother and me up at midnight, and then *every hour* on the hour after that, I'm going to make *you* a ghost!"

"But there's no such thing as ghosts," I corrected him.

"Damn right about that. Now go in your room and don't come out until you're in high school."

This is the earliest memory I have of my father, and probably the earliest he ever arose on a Saturday when he wasn't working in the oilfields.

The first movie ever to give me a nightmare was "The

Creeping Eye." It was a black and white movie, set in the Swiss Alps, I think, that showed the dangers of modern science and downhill skiing. A mutated eye was terrorizing the Swiss, who were apparently too busy making chocolate to see the slimy little orb come up on them and strangle them.

My memory fails me here. I don't know how an eye could strangle someone, but trust me, it was terrifying, at least to a four-year-old boy.

I spent most of my early childhood in fear of one thing or another; usually the afternoon creature features provided all the nightmare material I needed for weeks on end of fitful sleep. After several death threats from my father, which I found less frightening than "The Mummy," I learned to just stay in my room and scream. Mom would come in, and she was a lot more sympathetic, at least early on.

Even though he was just a baby, my brother Jim soon joined me in my afternoon obsession. He didn't know what to make of the TV, but he could tell from my face and posture just when to scream himself. It was usually when I crawled under the coil rug or hid behind Dad's recliner.

Monsters never know to look behind anything covered in Naugahyde, you see.

In a sense, I felt a lot safer in there with my brother. I figured the monsters would stop and eat him first, giving me time to get away. This was pretty much my method of self-preservation all through those early years, until my kid sister came along and then my brother and I *both* had another layer of insurance. We thought it was great that we had a little sister because monsters seem to eat the women first. The only men who got "ait" were those dumb enough to try and rescue someone, and we sure as heck weren't going to do *that*.

The afternoon horror shows got scarier and scarier, as we expanded our monster madness to include Dracula,

Frankenstein, Invasion of the Body Snatchers, and King Kong vs. Godzilla. The people in these Japanese movies had the amazing ability to talk, at times, without moving their mouths, and at other times they must have been scared speechless, as their mouths would flap and nothing much came out.

But in terms of terror, things really got intense when we got a color TV. We knew that blood is red, but to see it, when a vampire left his mark, well that's tons worse. And we just had to look away when the Mummy was strangling someone and her face turned blue. It was just *too* familiar—it looked *exactly* like our fourth-grade teacher's face.

Things got even worse when Pat came into the picture. Jim and I would be huddled in the den, watching TV without permission, and she'd tiptoe in and break out into screams.

I think all three of us peed our pants at the same time.

It was hard to get her to pipe down. She had a low-terror threshold. Not only did she scream at the monsters, she howled in fear at the used car commercials featuring Cal Worthington and his alligator-dog, Spot.

Mom would sometimes intervene with her drive-by, television-deprivation tactic. She'd stop in front of the screen at a super-intense moment and block our view. Then, when she walked on, the TV was *off*.

This was a real tension killer. It usually took our television set *eons* to warm up again.

Well, at least it seemed like that.

You could make a cup of coffee or take a bathroom break while you were waiting for the tube to get up to speed. And all this time, the picture was fuzzy and all the colors were off. Godzilla looked pink, not green, and King Kong was as menacing as our cocker spaniel, Babe.

The main problem with afternoon scary movies was *reruns*. Once you've seen a movie three or four hundred times, the hide-in-the-closet terror factor goes away. In fact, the movie becomes funny. You begin to notice things that you didn't the first few dozen times you'd seen it. The airplanes flying around Kong and the Empire State Building are the wrong size, and ant-sized people who looked *terrified* as the monster towered over them are, in close-ups, just limp little dolls.

Boring. Boring. Boring. So, Jim and I invented new diversions to throw new excitement into the mix—we made up stuff to annoy our sister.

This was a whole new area of fun, since Pat was so trusting, and at age 6, pretty gullible. We'd warn her that, after the huge explosion that was going to happen, she'd go deaf for a while. Then, we'd turn the volume on the TV all the way down, and Jim and I would mouth words back and forth to one another. When she'd ask us a question, we'd gesture wildly, flapping our lips to silently answer her.

This ruse lasted just up to the point where she'd call Mom in.

Another favorite trick, used more during fantasy than horror films, was to shine a flashlight on the wall, and tell her it was Tinkerbell, escaped from the TV and ready to grant a wish, if only we could catch her. Pat would race about the house, crawling over furniture and shelves, until she either broke something, got tired and fell asleep, or the flashlight batteries went dead.

These bonding moments with Pat were best done late at night, after Mom and Dad had gone to bed and we had the front room to ourselves. Of course we'd been sent to bed, but on Saturday nights, we'd sneak out and find Seymour, our guide to horrible horror films, or Elvira, in her slinky outfits, and watch the dregs of American cinema. We had to be careful to keep it down, or Dad would wake up, chew us all out, and send us to bed without the satisfaction of scaring Pat out of the room just as the movie ended.

But most of the time we managed to stifle our sister's screams with a well-tossed pillow or buy her off with some candy to stop the sniveling. Usually it worked. At other times we'd spin elaborate stories of how she could protect herself by setting up booby traps.

Each week we'd offer her another idea to protect herself. She learned, over time, to drag the large, swivel mounted mirror up to the back door. This would confuse the mummy. She'd set out pots and pans full of water to keep away the Cat People, or zigzag string through the room, anchoring it on the fireplace, coat rack, and rocking chair. This kept out the vampires when they traveled as bats, or she'd place garlic on the floor to keep them out when they were in human form. There was a small stack of silver bells near the sink, to ward off werewolves, and we even persuaded Pat that propping a bag of flour on the upper edge of the door would make the invisible man visible, and avoidable, if he happened in that way. We kept adding new traps, and delighted in how much work she put into setting them.

But, alas, all good things must come to an end, and our anti-monster tactics came to an abrupt halt one Halloween night.

***

It was a special evening—the last year I was young enough to do it and the first year Mom felt comfortable letting the three of us hit the neighborhood by ourselves. We had a great haul, mostly because we just kept holding our bags out, unabashedly, without our mother to tell us "that's enough," and reign in our greed.

We had to quit a bit early, because our bags were about to burst. But that was OK because Jim and I planned to enjoy Channel 13's all night *Fright Fest*. Naturally, our parent's had said no, but that was not an obstacle. And the major attraction wasn't the movies, it would be our sister's utter terror—we'd been building up her anxieties for *weeks*.

Mom and Dad tucked the three of us into bed, and we

waited about a half hour. We snuck into the hallway and cracked open the door to the den. It was a bit early, but it doesn't hurt to check.

And we were in luck! No trace of mom and dad. This meant we could start *much* earlier. All three of us crept into the den. I closed the door, and Jim turned on the TV.

We told Pat that she had a *lot* of work to do because all the spirits would be out, and that we feared for our lives.

So she spared no effort to protect herself and set up a full array of anti-monster countermeasure—with a bit of help from us—to ward off evil. She did *such* a good job that it was impossible to go from the den to the kitchen stove and pop popcorn. In fact, there were so many booby traps none of us could even reach the *bathroom*.

All this had been done in CIA-like silence. When Pat was done, Jim and I smiled at one another. We'd trained our sister well.

Or so we thought…

Sometime during Hitchcock's "The Birds," Pat screamed, and we were a bit slow in shutting her up. Jim and I listened, holding our breath, to see if the tell-tale thumping of my infuriated father's feet would head our way.

But we lucked out. We couldn't believe our good fortune when our sister screamed again, a piercing and lingering wail, and Dad still failed to materialize.

It was in the final moments of the movie that, just as the victims were making one last desperate attempt to save themselves, that the TV went dead and the room blacked. We heard a low moan by the back door.

The back door flew open, and a huge, silhouetted figure dashed in, slamming into the mirror and sending it crashing to the floor. All three of us gasped and then formed a three-part harmony of screams.

The figure staggered sideways, stepping into the pots and pans full of water, sloshing it everywhere and sliding into the web of twine that ran throughout the front room.

My sister may have been only six years old, but she could tie a good knot, and the twine held fast to the fireplace. The rapidly moving phantom slid on an collision course with the wooden rocker, and connected with one of the chair's sharp edges in that region of the body that lies just below the belly button. A sharp, un-Mummylike cry came from the creature.

But like any good monster, though, this thing kept coming at us. The coat rack clock gave its all trying to save us, and toppled down on the rocker just as the creature stood up, knocking it back to the floor and burying it in polyester and fleece.

The immobile monster moaned, and then began to curse. These were not the sort of curses that a witch might make, but something much more familiar and closer to home.

"*Uh-oh,*" said Jim.

"Daddy?" said Pat.

I didn't say *anything*. It occurred to me that in the dark, I might be able to get back to my bedroom before the lights came on, and pretend to be asleep.

While I was contemplating this move, I heard another sound that cut me off dead in my tracks. It was a not-so-loud thumping in the hallway, coming rapidly in our direction.

The door to the front room flew open, and in an instant, a bag of flour rained down on my mother's head. She cried out like a cat with a freshly crushed tail. The door opened wide to reveal her, flashlight in hand, surrounded by a cloud of white dust.

Mom took a step toward forward, but her foot came down on a garlic clove, and she hobbled to the counter, snagging the small stack of bells. It sounded for a moment, like Christmas had come early, and Frosty the Snowman was ringing his way to town.

The creature on the floor quit cursing, and, miraculously, started to laugh.

Mom saved the night, in more ways than one, as none of us were thrashed. She told Dad that if he hadn't been so intent on scaring us with his prank, none of this would have happened.

In other words, it was *his fault*. Hurrah!

Her other act of generosity—Mom didn't hold my sister responsible for all the booby traps.

But Jim and I were not *quite* so lucky. We had to clean the whole mess up. We were forever barred from watching monster films, which, of course, meant that we had to wait almost two months before the next creature feature.

But I was given the worst punishment of all. I was forced to sit down early that next morning, and draw crude pictures on the kitchen message board, to try and convince my sister that, really, "there's no such things as ghosts."

twenty two

LITTLE SHOP OF HORRORS

Dad was never happier than when he'd been shopping at
Sears.

"Power tools," he said, "are proof that God exists, and
that he loves us." He was fondling his new cobalt-blue drill
with a faraway look in his eyes. Was he dreaming of all the
projects that were now possible? Would the drill help him
finish tasks that, just days before, had eluded him?

I saw him smile in ecstasy.

"Watch this," he said, and snapped a small whetstone
into the chuck. He spat on it, and then proceeded to hold
the drill in one hand and his buck knife in the other.

"Shouldn't you clamp the knife in a vise?" I asked, as
sparks showered on his boots.

"You sound like your mother," he said, glancing up
with a grin.

In that instant the drill bobbled and its chuck caught
the knife's leather strap, flinging it across the garage and
impaling it in Mom's ironing board.

We exchanged looks. Dad stowed the drill, and strode
over to recover his knife. He resembled a modern-day

Arthur, grasping Excalibur's handle and claiming the blade. The fact that he and—he alone—could do this stunt proved he was king of his small domain.

He thumbed the blade.

"Perfect," he said. Then he added, "You don't need to tell Mom about this."

It was one of those father-and-son moments where we briefly united by a common fear of getting chewed out. I took the opportunity to ask him if I could try out his tools.

He held up a gnarled hand.

"Nope, not until you're older."

"But Dad," I pleaded.

"I'll tell you what," he said. "It's OK with me when it's OK with your mother."

"Really?"

"Sure." He motioned to the house. "Why don't you ask her?"

I dashed into the house, and found Mom mending my sister's pants. She had a thimble on one finger, and was absorbed in her work.

"Can I?" I gasped. "Dad says it's OK with him if it's OK with you."

"OK to do what?"

I had to think about this question for a moment. I didn't want to make anything more than a few holes in a piece of scrap wood. I wasn't sure how to sell her on the virtues of sawdust.

"Oh, you know, guy stuff?"

At this, she looked up.

"Such as?"

"Drill some holes, and …"

"No."

"Or, maybe…"

"No."

"But Mom."

"No."

"But he'll show me how to do it."

"That's why the answer is no."

And that was that. So, for years woodworking at my house was a spectator sport. I must say, it wasn't dull. Dad's love for tools was often unrequited. They didn't seem to love him back. More than once I saw him emerge from the shop holding a bloody rag to some body part. He didn't believe in using safety gear, and the last time he read instructions, Eisenhower was president.

Mom, if she was around, either dashed to him to offer aid, or if he was not too badly hurt, waved a spoon and gave him a piece of her mind. Between dealing with Dad and me, it was amazing that she had any sanity left. She begged, she pleaded, and she lectured, to no avail.

"You'll be the death of me," she would tell Dad, or "I'll be a widow yet." I wasn't sure how Dad was going to kill her at the same time he killed himself, but if anyone could do it, it would be Rotarysaw Ronnie.

But Dad viewed his injuries as no more than a brief time-out. Mom, his personal trainer, would administer generous quantities of iodine and yards and yards of gauze. She seemed to think that she could protect him from further harm with generous cushions of cotton. Usually, once the bleeding stopped, Dad just peeled off the dressings and was back in the game. But, while on the bench, Dad endured Mom's coaching.

"Really, Ronald," she'd begin. "You do have goggles, gloves, and safety guards."

"Aw, that stuff just gets in the way," he'd say, and laugh. "Besides, it's just like in the scriptures…sometimes you've got to make a blood sacrifice."

"That's not funny," she said and gave him *the look*.

Dad called these lectures, after Mom left the room, "Sister Martha's Sunday-school sermons." He heard them so many times that he gave them numbers. One day when I came back from a bike ride, he was sitting at the kitchen table, a bandage over one eye. He looked at me and said, "Number five."

"Number five?" I asked.

"'Thou shall not grind without goggles,'" he said.

Later that day, he was standing in the bathroom, digging into his palm with a pair of tweezers.

He didn't look up as I walked by, but he spoke to me:

"Number 12, 'Thou shall wear work gloves in the garage.'"

I looked at Dad, with his bloody bandage, and wondered what sermons six through eleven covered.

For the longest time, I figured that this was all part of making and fixing things. I thought that you'd open a book on how to make a bookcase, and step number eight would be how to administer a tourniquet while still applying the lacquer finish. I longed to enter the manly world of woodworking. But Mom stood firm.

Finally, I entered middle school and signed up for 7th grade wood shop.

I felt a surge of confidence entering the classroom. I assumed that I knew all there was about woodworking. But for the first three weeks, we did nothing but go over all the safety precautions. Proper gear, proper clothing, proper use of the tools. I was properly bored out of my mind. True, it was all new to me, since I'd never seen dad do any of this stuff.

After an eternity, I was allowed to use the tools. Our first project—using the router to make a hot plate.

I took it home to show my Mom and Dad.

"Well," Mom said. "This will be very useful." She ran her hand over the grooves, feeling the texture of the pine. The wooden disk still smelled of Linseed oil. "We'll have to keep this on the counter where everyone can see it." She smiled.

I beamed, proud of my first creation.

Dad took it from her, and flipped it over in his hands a couple of times, like it was a pancake. He rolled it along the kitchen table.

"Almost perfect, son."

"Almost?" My face fell.

"Looks like it's missing something," Dad said, shaking his head sadly.

"What?" I asked.

He held it up close to his nose and squinted.

"No blood stains."

twenty three

THE PUDDLE-JUMPER'S APOLOGY

My mother's joy bloomed anew each rainstorm. She'd grown up on the damp Gulf Coast of Texas, Corpus Christi to be exact, and she missed the rain. After marrying Dad, and moving to Oildale, the only cloud-like shapes Mom saw rolling across the horizon were tumbleweeds. We had plenty of those.

Rain was a rarity in Oildale. But Mom never lost faith it would come. The sound of it rattling on the shed's tin roof, the smell of it settling all the dust, the feel of it splattering on a window sill and fizzing up into your face, these all put her in a "have a second piece of pie" mood.

Mom used to say that rain was magic, and without rain you don't get rainbows.

"You learn something important about people by the way they handle rain. Without rain, there'd be no food, no flowers, and no silver linings at the end of the day."

Dad saw every drop that fell as trouble with a big, black overcoating. "No good has ever come of rain." He countered Mom's joy with wet-blanket pessimism. "Noah can keep it."

133

As long as Dad could turn on the tap and get water for his coffee and the occasional shower, he had all he needed. For him, rain at his work in the oilfields meant slippery steel walkways near the open mouths of tanks, full of boiling oil, and only an angle-iron grab rail between you and a 30-foot-deep well of hot crude. Rain meant gooey roads, stuck tanker trucks, and the risk of fire from slipping belts on oil pumps out in the 7th Standard roundhouses. Rain was to be endured, until it passed.

For me, as usual, rain meant a trip to the principal's office. I had been demonstrating the art of jumping in a puddle without getting wet when Pam had wobbled by in her galoshes, too slowly and entirely too close, wearing the new sweater and skirt she'd gotten for her birthday.

Timing is everything, especially when it comes to dealing with puddles. Poor Pam had a *terrible* sense of timing. She managed to get herself wet just as the yard monitor rounded the corner. Mrs. Glidewell didn't even break her stride as she grabbed me in one fluid motion and slid me down to Mr. Lewis' office. She managed to plow through several puddles, soaking my shoes. It did get me to the principal's office in a flash, but it blunted the message of how it was "not a nice thing to get people wet."

Once in the office, I pointed out that I hadn't intended to get Pam wet; I'd been angling for my buddy Chris. But that didn't seem to matter to Mr. Lewis. I asked Mr. Lewis what he thought about Mrs. Glidewell dragging me through mud puddles, on purpose. He frowned, looked at me, picked up a stack of folders on his desk, opened one with my name on it, and made a red mark inside. He then straightened the stack, sat it down, and asked me what I'd like to do with the rest of my recess.

"I'd like to play in the rain."

"Do you think you can stay away from puddles?"

I flinched. Rain puddles were a rarity, a resource to be exploited. "Maybe."

He sighed. "Can you find Pam and apologize?"

This, I promised, I could do. I might have to run all over the playground and back, but I'd be sure to find her before the bell rang. Thus bound by my promise, I dashed off in pursuit.

I looped around the playground three times, sliding through or skirting puddles as the mood moved me. After surfing across the basketball courts, I did find Pam, and gave her a limp apology.

"How come you were standing so close to my mud puddle?" I opened. There were no adults present, and I didn't want to give too much ground.

"I wasn't standing anywhere," she said with a scowl. Her sweater was still wet from where she'd had to rinse it out. "You ran up and splashed me."

"Ah, well," I looked over towards the swings and saw Mrs. Glidewell watching the two of us. She couldn't see Pam's face, and I was pretty sure Mrs. G was too far away to hear me, but I knew that I needed to get this done without having Pam run away screaming mad, again. "Ah, yeah. I guess I... I am...."

Pam looked expectantly at me.

The bell rang, and I wondered if that meant I was off the hook. I decided, as Mrs. Glidewell began walking our way that I wasn't. "I am sorry you were there, near the puddle."

"Me too," Pam said, looking hurt.

Now I really did feel bad. It was one thing to disappoint Mr. Lewis and Mrs. G, but Pam? Well, she'd always been kind of nice.

"I mean, it was not right," I continued. "A mistake."

Mrs. Glidewell stepped up before I could say more.

"You did hear the bell," Mrs. G looked past Pam and squarely at me.

"I was just apologizing," I mumbled.

"That's good," she said, smiling.

"Yeah," I said, finding my full voice. "Mr. Lewis was telling me how it isn't nice to get people wet on purpose."

I looked Mrs. G dead in the eye, and her smile went away.

"We all need to get to our classrooms." Mrs. G tapped the top of Pam's head and put her hand firmly in my back with a solid push towards Mr. Kidd's room.

***

My sixth-grade teacher Mr. Kidd loved the rain. He was the rare person who relished being trapped in a room with 30 kids. It was a chance for him to work his particular teaching methods.

For example, Mr. Kidd was quick to recognize each child's individuality and unique characteristics. My classmate Hughie complained that he had a cold, and asked if he could have a tissue off Mr. Kidd's desk. This request was denied, until Hughie began wiping his nose on his sleeve. Then, Mr. Kidd dubbed Hughie "The Nose," and gave him his own personal box of Kleenex, and a "snot bucket" that consisted of an empty coffee can. Mr. Kidd made a point of banging into this can each time he went by, and making a face, saying "Eeeaagh!" This caused the class to laugh, and Hughie-the-Nose to cringe and make a renewed effort to quit sniffling.

Then there was Howie. Howie had his own problem, which consisted of uncontrollable itching. Howie's mom had insisted that he wear a woolen sweater, on account of the rain, and poor Howie kept trying to scratch his back. Mr. Kidd "helped" him by giving him a new name, "Scratchy," and Mr. Kidd presented Scratchy-Howie with the 4-foot long pointer, normally used to direct our attention to the map of the world. The pointer was too long for Howie to use, so Mr. Kidd gave it to Bev, the girl who sat behind Howie. Bev was told to help Howie, anytime he seemed to be itchy, and then she was free to poke him.

The lesson behind all this was not lost on the rest of the class. And most of the rest of them suffered in silence.

This was not news to me, though. I had, long before this, been awarded my own class moniker for talking excessively. Mr. Kidd called me the "Tongue."

Aside from giving people nicknames, Mr. Kidd was an expert in gamesmanship. I don't remember the class curriculum, but I do remember his ability to invent activities to amuse himself. The new game that Mr. Kidd introduced that rainy day was "Lost Child." The idea is that one person was sent outside, in the rain, while the rest of the class scrambled about, each person landing in someone else's seat. One child was hidden in the clothes closet. The guesser came back in and had one hint, two minutes, and three guesses to figure out who was missing.

Everyone wanted to volunteer for either the lost child or the guesser. And I waved my arm enthusiastically, but was ignored. Time and again, as we passed the hour just before lunch, we picked the lucky two. I was skipped. I began to howl, "Not Fair! Not Fair!" when Mr. Kidd began to give people second or third turns. Mr. Kidd looked at me, smirked, and said, to no one in particular: "The Tongue can't be still for two minutes!"

Finally, with less than five minutes to lunch, I jumped up, and belted out "Me! Me!" Mr. Kidd ignored me, and picked Susan to go outside and wait. Then, Mr. Kidd waved his arms, and we all scrambled. I shuffled to Susan's desk, and slumped into her seat. I was amazed when Mr. Kidd walked over, with his finger to his lips, looked me in the eye, and pointed to the closet. I was going to be the lost child. Fantastic!

The class still was rattling with activity as I dove in the closet and buried myself amid the jackets and umbrellas. The rustling continued, muted by all the heavy clothing. I heard the door open and Susan's muffled voice, and then the noise slowly died down. I heard a giggle, and then no more.

I sat and waited. Stifling my own desire to giggle or laugh with joy. Time is hard to judge when sitting in the dark, compressed into a small space. But within a short while, I began to have trouble breathing. Asthma. I was horrified that I would start wheezing, a sad tell-tale trademark, and give myself away. I held my breath, and lost all sense of time. I felt the buttons from Mr. Kidd's jacket dig into my face. I tried to look at my Mickey Mouse watch, but it was just too dark. So I waited.

I decided that I could measure time in my own way by counting, and I was proud of myself that I figured out that I needed to count to 120 before, surely, the door would fly open and I would jump out just like they do on those TV game shows.

I was good in math, but I'd never needed to count that high to play a game. Hide and seek topped out at either 25 or 100, depending on whether we played by Sam's rules or Chris' rules. I never was brave enough to ask, but I don't think Sam could count much past 25. It was one of those questions you don't put to people twice your size.

So I counted to pass the time. And I decided I'd do it right: "One-Mississippi, two-Mississippi...." and I wondered who decided it should be "Mississippi" and not "California" or even "Tennessee?" I worked through this mystery, and then reached 120. There was total silence on the other side of the room, and I thought that seemed odd. But there were a lot of coats in the closet, and I didn't want to lose by giving myself away. I kept waiting for Mr. Kidd's booming voice saying: "Nope. You're a loser."

But after counting, and then again by twos and threes, I had to admire how thoroughly we'd been able to stump Susan. She couldn't figure it out, and we'd beat her! I decided it was time to crack the door open to see the expression on her face when she bombed out.

The door didn't make a sound as I eased it open, and looked through slit. I squinted in the suddenly bright light, but couldn't spot Susan. Then it dawned on me that I couldn't see *anyone*. The room was empty.

I stepped out of the closet and looked across a

cluttered mess of desks abandoned in a moment of gleeful opportunity. I realized that over at the cafeteria, 29 small kids and one very large one were laughing their heads off over hotdogs, fish sticks, and creamed corn.

I donned my coat, and pushed out into the outdoor hallway. It was five past noon, and I had managed to wait more than 10 minutes, a record of sorts. I wasn't feeling any sense of victory, though, for outlasting Mr. Kidd's prediction. I shuffled over to the cafeteria, and I was greeted by a chorus of hoots and laughter at my expense. To make matters worse, they had run out of hot dogs and all they had left were fish sticks.

I walked over to the line, falling in behind the fifth graders, who had been briefed, too, and were laughing at me, when I saw a small figure standing, a bit apart from the crowd, and motioning me over. It was Pam, and she had an extra tray of food.

That day was the first time I ever sat down to eat lunch with a girl, on purpose, who wasn't my Mom. Pam said that it was mean what they did to me, and that she had thought about it and knew I hadn't intended to splash her. She told me that she accepted my apology.

Mom was right. The rain can bring out the best and the worst in people. I was lucky that day that I managed to see someone in a whole new way, and I didn't care at all that Chris and Sam made fun of me for being a sissy and sitting with the girls.

I *did* make sure that the next time there was a huge puddle, that it was the two of them, and not Pam, who earned me a trip to the principal's office.

twenty four

BIKINI

For the first 11 years of my life, I imagined that all women were, more or less, subtle variations of my mother.

Then came the first day of summer of '66, when I saw *Bikini*.

She was watering her front lawn, just standing there, backlit by the sun, with water dripping off her body from where she's hosed herself down in the heat. I stopped my bicycle and stared.

I'd never seen anything like this before. Not on television, not in any of our "Highlights" magazines, not even at our community pool. I thought that women's bathing suits were all like the ones Mom and Grandma wore—one big stretchy piece of material that was reluctantly worn underneath two-layers of towels and a terry-cloth bath robe.

But something quite unreluctant was in plain view at 1065 Day Street. It was history in the making, and the semi-regular 5:45 pm *watering her lawn* became the talk of the neighborhood.

It was a secret at first. The men coming home from

their oilfield jobs spotted her while their wives where laboring over the stove, putting dinner together.

Soon the locker rooms all around town had just one topic of conversation, and for a while men eagerly ran errands to Safeway or Miller's Variety in the early evening—a time most of them would normally be glued to their Barcaloungers after a long, gritty day in the heat.

Then disaster struck. My mother's best friend Alice happened to decline her husband's eager offer to fetch dinner fixings. Fred pleaded, but there's no fooling with Alice once she makes up her mind. She was, though, touched by her husband's insistence, and so she invited him along. Strangely, Fred grunted, shook his head, and then shuffled off to his recliner.

Alice drove herself to Safeway, puzzled. She was daydreaming a bit, reflecting on her husband's strange behavior, and she almost rear-ended Sam O'Neill's Chevy, stopped in the middle of Day Street. Her eyes followed his rapt stare toward the lawn of "1065", across the wet-arc of spray and back to its source. Then, in an instant, Alice managed to put 36, 24, and 32 together.

That was the end of Fred's afternoon trips to Safeway.

And, of course, Alice told my mom, who told Mavis, who told Sally and Marge. For the next two hours the town was one big busy signal as female friend called female friend, friends called acquaintances, and acquaintances even called women they disliked in the face of a major threat.

By the end of that day, and thereafter, the traffic on Day Street eased up considerably.

The men still talked, and I caught snatches of conversation that were more mysterious than the bikini-clad woman herself.

"Divorcee," Bill declared.

"Airline Stewardess," Roy countered.

The local highway patrolman, who seemed to know the workings of the town better than anyone else, had the most interesting story: "A 'professional,' if you know what I mean...."

I didn't, but it was great stuff, and the boys of the neighborhood began to share in the mystery that was "Bikini." We found new reasons to bicycle past "1065," even when she wasn't around. The house itself became a sort of shrine.

The sensation of the summer of '62 was only a few weeks old, when the contractor's trucks arrived, and two feet were added to the top of the cinder block fence that surrounded her yard.

The locker rooms rattled with spicy speculation.

"That proves it," Ed nodded.

"No tan lines," Will leered.

"Naked as a jay bird," Sonny smiled.

In the kitchens and laundry rooms, the women linked up by telephone with a different take on the topic.

"Who does she think she is?" Alice asked.

"It's immoral," Mavis snorted.

The summer temperatures may have been in the high 90s, but inside the dens and bedrooms of Oildale, the men were finding things downright frosty.

Now, the men lived in a different world from the boys, and my friends and I faced no such problems or travel restrictions. Youthful innocence has its advantages.

Some of us were more innocent than others, though, and it was Sam Young who educated me by way of proving how *manly* and *with it* he was. We were standing behind the 7-11, looking at the two new layers of cinder blocks on the back wall of "1065."

"You know why they added those blocks?" he leered.

"Ah, sure," I said.

"Liar! Then tell me."

I rummaged through the bits of the rumor mill that I'd heard. "She's got a cat. That's what I hear. A really bad cat that can't be allowed out."

Sam mulled this over, and smiled.

"Boy, you're a dumb little kid."

"Am *not*!"

"I'll bet you haven't even seen a *Playboy* Magazine."

"Sure have!"

"Right," Sam shook his head.

"Yes I have. We have boxes of them."

"Boxes? No one has boxes of them."

"We do. My dad has every one ever printed," I said, "and *two* copies of the good ones."

Sam smiled wickedly. "Then you'd know all about nude sunbathing," he said.

"Sure. They had a big article on it last week, with coupons for free soap."

Sam doubled over, laughing.

"Look, dummy, nude sunbathing is lying in the sun with no clothes on," Sam explained.

"Oh… right."

They say that great moments in personal growth often come in bursts of illumination, and that the facts of the moment are fixed in your mind, forever.

I can remember clearly that it was 5:45, and there was no sign of her on the front lawn. The two top rows of cinder blocks were a salmon pink, and Sam and I could hear music in her back yard. Sinful songs, top-40 rock tunes bounced over the fence. We imagined—as best we could—the sounds sliding out of the radio, across the patio, over the bronzed, topless, form of Bikini, and then floating in ecstasy over that wall and toward us. We listened carefully, to see if the music somehow sounded different for having been in such intimate contact with Bikini.

Sam and I lingered in the alley. Beads of sweat formed on our foreheads and dripped into little puddles on the ground.

While we stood there, Chris Olson pedaled up and looked the two of us over.

"You know," Chris paused and took a long pull from

his blue Slurpee, "that she answers her door topless, too."

"No way!" Sam and I both yelled.

"Yep." He nodded. "Will told me that Fred told him that he'd overheard Ed the postal carrier saying that Sam who covers this route had told him so."

"Topless?" Sam asked.

"Well, wrapped in a towel but topless," Chris said.

"Wow. How did Sam know, uh, if there was that towel?"

Chris rolled his eyes. "You ever see a Playboy, right?"

"Ah… sure…." Sam said.

"Well, then you know."

Now there were three of us immobilized, replenishing the groundwater supply with the sweat that was pouring off us. We squinted into the sun, staring intently at that fence, willing ourselves to have superhero, X-Ray vision.

It didn't work.

I don't remember if it was Chris' idea, or Sam's—they both blamed me later. But most of the really bad ideas in my life originated in other people's brains. They just seemed to get stuck in mine. But we all agreed, after our brains had been bleached out, that we'd get her to answer the door and see for ourselves.

A smarter or a nicer group of boys might have donned their Cub Scout uniforms and tried selling magazine subscriptions or gathering Coke bottles door to door, as a cover. Since these sorts of operations never make any money, they're always really a ruse for casing the neighborhood.

But we were not nice, and as it turns out we weren't very smart either.

Someone suggested that we use the "ring and run" approach to surveillance.

For those people who grew up in better neighborhoods or without the edifying experience of young boys in the household, your "ring and run" approach is to ring the doorbell, or knock if you must, and run like hell.

It also is considered good form to hide in the bushes.

This latter approach would have been preferred, but there was no suitable landscaping to support this tactic.

So, we decided to have one of us, to be determined by lot, ring the bell, and run. The others got to hang out across the alley, behind the 7-11, and watch the doorway. This meant that the person who did the ringing and running would not really get much of a view. Unlike our mothers, none of us had eyes in the back of our heads. So, losing the toss meant taking all the risk for no benefit.

Sam eagerly produced his lucky silver dollar. I had long suspected that Sam had a two-headed coin. He'd win all the tosses, no matter what, and he'd never let you touch his dollar.

I suggested that we Ro-sham-bo for our fate. Sam wasn't sure that this was the sort of major life decision that should be made by paper-rock-scissors.

"You've gotta be kidding," Sam said.

"What's wrong with Ro-sham-bo?" I asked.

"You're going to look back on this day and realize the first time you got to see it for real you did it with scissors?"

He had me there. I did tend to favor scissors. Still, I was pondering the hidden wisdom of this statement, when Chris weighed in on my side.

"We have to do paper-rock-scissors because there's three of us."

Fortunately, Sam had to agree because Chris was the smartest one of the lot, and anyway it was two against one, even if Sam was the biggest kid in the neighborhood.

He slipped his lucky coin back into his pocket.

I was pretty nervous when we did Ro-sham-bo. I wanted to go for paper, but did scissors out of habit.

But I got lucky. I guess Sam figured that I wouldn't do scissors because he knew I would. So, I won and Sam lost. Chris was second with the best two out of three.

That's how it was that Sam had to do the dirty deed. I felt a bit sorry for him, but there was the chance that he could reach the cover of the dumpster. This left Chris and I to see what no boy had seen before.

Sam strode over, never looking back, and pounded on the door like a police officer, and then ran towards us, shrieking. He made the shelter of the dumpster, and then... nothing.

We waited.

"Maybe she's not home," Chris said.

"Her car's there," Sam answered.

It was true her red Fiat sports car was in the driveway, top down, but that was the only sign of her. I was looking at the car and pondering, when Chris called out.

"The door!"

I looked, but it was closed.

"It opened just a bit, and then it closed. I saw her face!"

"Was she?"

"I just saw her face."

"Was she... naked?"

"How should I know?"

What to do now? As we'd been taught in Cub Scouts: try, try again.

Chris was next up, and he was the smallest of us, but the fastest by far. The sound of his bell-ringing had hardly finished before he was beside us again, panting, as we all were.

This time, the door opened much sooner, and much wider. Bikini stepped out, towels wrapped about her hips and torso, with a hand holding each precariously in place. She stepped barefooted down the stairs, looking left and right.

We dove behind the dumpster, and peeked out.

She stood there a moment or two, and then stomped back in, slamming the door.

"OK," said Sam. "We need to do this one more time and see if we can get those towels off?"

It was, of course, my turn. Ringing the bell was no problem. But how to get the towels off? I hadn't a clue.

"So, what do we do?"

"We? It's your turn buddy-boy," Sam said.

He pointed towards the door, and suddenly it looked as inviting as a machine-gun nest. I stared at the button I was to press, just a few yards away, and willed my legs to take me there. They didn't at first, until Sam gave me a big push in the back, and I scurried up to the welcome mat.

I hesitated, glancing back at my grinning friends and pondering whether I should ring or knock. Both had been done, to no good effect. But ringing at least allowed me to push off the wall for my escape. I rang, and was in the process of turning to sprint, when the door flew open, and a very angry, semi-mummified form appeared. I can't say that she greeted me, in the usual sense of the word.

For a full description of what happened, I have to rely on the observations of my hidden accomplices, a term chosen by those who later documented this event.

I took off, arms pumping, and Bikini pursued. I had the initial advantage, not of surprise, for that belonged to her alone, but of dread, fear, and a few feet head start.

Unfortunately for me, this advantage was soon overtaken by that of a much taller, much angrier person who wielded a wooden yardstick. This yardstick was brought down, in one sweeping motion, on my head.

Since I wasn't looking back, only listening to her screaming commands: "Stop, you little brat!"

I didn't hear the slicing sound and fury of 36 inches of justice.

The smack on the side of my head put me into overdrive, and I managed, by degrees, to pull away from her.

For a brief time, I considered myself lucky. I was wearing my baseball cap, and this took most of the sting out of the blow. The cap flew off, but it had done its work. I managed to cut across a neighbor's yard, through a row of bushes, and doubled back to the 7-11. My friends were nowhere in sight. But I was safe, and I had a story to tell.

I walked cautiously, looking over my back, all the way to Sam's house, but he wasn't there, and I was watching my backside when I made it to Chris' place. He, too, was lying low.

So, it seemed only sensible to return home and nurse the bump on my head. I was eager to hear the reports of just what my buddies had seen. I'd been too busy saving my skin to know if the towels had stayed in place during my brief pursuit. I was hopeful, since her hands were clearly involved in pummeling me, but I figured I would phone Sam and Chris and get the whole story later.

Usually, my return home was unheralded, shrouded by the din of my younger siblings. My dog was there to greet me as I came in the back door.

The house was quiet, not even the TV was on. Strange.

"Robb. Robb Lane Lightfoot, come in here."

The middle name. Oh boy, that's bad news.

I shuffled into the front room, and I saw my mother. I also saw the back of a tall woman in a flowery dress. My mother was holding my baseball cap.

Over the years, I'd never thought that much about my mother's dedication to labeling and stenciling my underwear and clothing. It made sense, when it came to going to camp. She had that vain hope I'd return with all the towels and clothing I left with. Other than that, it was a mystery to me why she was so dedicated to labeling all my clothes. I thought that maybe, if I had some terrible bike accident, she'd be able to identify the remains because of my properly-labeled underwear.

But there was that baseball cap, probably the only cap in the entire world with an ID label sewed into it. Why hadn't I thought about this? Because I didn't know it was there. Honestly, who even *looks* inside the sweat band of a baseball cap? I can answer that question: mothers and women who wear bikini bathing suits do, that's who.

The interrogation was brief—there wasn't any denying what happened. And the follow-up investigation netted both Chris and Sam. Justice won out, just like on Dragnet.

My friends were mad at me for ratting them out, but the truth is I didn't say *anything*. I held to our code of silence. It didn't matter, though, because Mom knew enough to call *their* mothers. They were busted and got a visit from Bikini, too.

Actually, I paid an even bigger price for holding out. When I was asked who rang the bell before me, I said I'd heard that the postman always rings twice…. This, my mother said, was not a "satisfactory" answer, and I was denied TV for a month.

Worse still was what Sam and Chris did to me. They decided they'd *never* reveal what they saw when I was being chased by Bikini. Later, they did admit she was wearing a bathrobe, but their ever-changing hints and innuendos made it sound like her garments may have dissolved in her hot pursuit of me.

I never knew.

The lump on my head kept me from getting the electric chair, though. My mother was in her "wait until your father gets home" mode, and was holding the point of my chin, to ensure eye contact, when she noticed the knot on my temple. She studied it, and my injury was a pretty good-sized goose egg. I winced, and admitted that I'd gotten that in the process of getting my hat knocked off. My mother called Miss Moore, aka Bikini, and learned that she'd broken a yardstick over my head.

It's funny how you can lose a battle and win a war. That blow, deserved as it was, colored my mother's perception of the event. She put some Bactine on the abrasion, and interceded with my father more than she incited him. I was hovering near my bedroom door, and caught bits of her conversation:

"He's already been punished…."

"I called the other parents."

My father *di*d come in my room, and ask me how my day was. I mumbled something about messing up and

149

getting in trouble. He was acting really weird. I was sure I'd get another thrashing from him, but he just smiled, and never said another word about it.

And that was it. Absolutely and completely, at least for me, anyway.

Sam and Chris went on to cult fame, a sort of the grade-school equivalent of selling their story to the tabloids. I never heard about it directly from them. It was odd, hearing a story about me that I'd not witnessed. Various accounts had her wrapped in seven veils, being stark naked, except for thongs, and breaking a bat over my head, rendering me unconscious.

I couldn't dispute any of these, partly because my mother had forbidden me to talk about it.

***

The final chapter to this story occurred when I was home from college, nearly ten years later, having my wisdom teeth pulled.

I was nervous and waiting in the dentist's office feeling a combination of fear and a throbbing pain. Enter Ms. Moore—the dentist. Her hair was shorter. Her face had some laugh lines. But it was definitely her. She was wearing a loose-fitting lab coat, and standing there larger than life. I looked her over from the corner of my eye, and she still looked ... hot.

Dr. Moore glanced at me, then at the chart, quietly studying the X-rays that had been mailed to her, and smiled. I figured she had long since forgotten about me and my insatiable curiosity.

But I was wrong. She crossed the room in two large steps, grabbed my chin, and just before jabbing me with a needle, told me to "count backwards from 1065." Then the medication kicked in, my eyes crossed, and I blacked out faster than you can say "Ro-sham-bo."

When I came to, she was gone, and I was left drooling

in a chair with a bandage on my head. History repeats itself in strange ways.

My mother drove me home from this ordeal. I was able to mumble through the gauze packing in my mouth that I'd seen Ms. Moore—Dr. Moore—again.

"So," Mom said, feigning surprise. "How is the good doctor?"

"Just the same," I said, leaning back and feeling woozy. "No tan lines."

twenty five

THE DAY I GOT PADDLED AT SCHOOL

In most normal people, there is a filter that sits between their mouths and wild, spontaneous, and possibly anti-social thoughts. It's called the pre-frontal cortex, and I'm told it can be quite helpful in keeping you out of trouble.

In kindergarten, I was told some helpful hints on how to behave properly. Mostly, these were kind suggestions such as "count to 10 before you say anything." Of course, I didn't yet know how to count past five, and I think my parents were hoping that I might wait a few additional years before I said *anything* at all. Mom used to introduce my little brother Jim and me by saying. "Here's my youngest son 'Pete,' and my older son, 'Repeat.'"

For several years, I thought this was part of my given name, sort of like those long Italian or Latino Christian names that don't always show up fully on your birth certificate.

Life has a way of repeating itself, too, and so through all of grade school I found out that while I loved to talk, not everyone loved to listen. Listening is a virtue, of course; someone has to do it so the rest of us can talk.

More than one teacher informed me that they were the ones who were getting paid to talk, and so they often found it necessary to remove me as a source of competition. I spent many long hours in the Highland Elementary School office, at my own special desk that they'd brought in just for me, so I'd have a place to sit while waiting to converse with the principal. Usually, this wasn't as bad as it seems. He actually did talk to me, and listened as often as not, which is much more than I can say for my grade school teachers.

In third grade, Mrs. Glidewell did listen, and that seemed to be an improvement, until I found out that there are "socially unacceptable" words and thoughts. My growing vocabulary included things I'd heard my dad's truck-driving buddies say in casual conversations—four-letter words that I won't repeat here.

Some words had immense power. They caused Mrs. Glidewell to gasp, go red in the face, and implement a two-step punishment for the offense. I was to stop and wash my mouth out before reporting to the principal.

I learned the soap in our school may have had some redeeming qualities, but taste wasn't one of them. Also, later in the day, I found that this really was a "two step" punishment. I found that soap has additional properties which are not often listed in those Dove commercials on TV. Mrs. Glidewell managed to get rid of me without bothering the principal, as I spent recess in the boy's restroom.

On one or two occasions there was a special effort made, with my best interest in mind, to redirect my behavior. One in particular sticks out. On that fateful day, Mom was home sick in bed with the flu and a high fever, unable to get out of bed or even talk on the telephone. Dad took time off work to watch over her. This was most unusual, and his presence upset the normal household routine, which included the daily call from Mrs. Earl in the principal's office. She'd phone to report on what I'd said or done in class.

"I wanted to let you know that Robb was talking in class today, so we're keeping him after school for an hour," she said.

"Again?" Dad said.

Mrs. Earl was taken back by my dad's surprise. These phone calls had gone out daily for years, and this was the first time she'd encountered anything other than loving fortitude on the other end of the line. She must have sensed a rare opportunity.

"I'm afraid so, sir. We're really at our wit's end here."

"Well, why don't you just thrash him?" Dad said.

"Corporal punishment?" Mrs. Earl gasped. Since Dr. Spock's teachings of just five year's prior, no enlightened person spanked their kids anymore. Mom forbade Dad spanking me, and she had *never* suggested it to the school. But Mom was down for the count, and newly domestic Dad was calling the shots.

"Yeah. Just whack him," Dad said. "You've got my blessings." With that, he hung up, and the normal and routine administrative processes for handling me suddenly shifted into a whole new groove.

Of course, I knew nothing of what was about to happen.

So, instead of just waiting the afternoon away, my afternoon routine, I was called into the office, and told to stand just the left of Mr. Lewis' desk.

"Robb," Mr. Lewis began. "We are going to try something different today to deal with this problem." "This problem" was his shorthand for the daily visits.

"OK." I said brightly. I was tired of losing my afternoons to waiting around, and this sounded promising.

"Very well," he said, avoiding my eyes and instead looking down in his desk drawer. He slid it way, way out to reveal a row of wooden objects, each neatly fitted into a slot in a tray. For several seconds he said nothing, while I looked at these beautiful, shiny ... paddles.

"Oh?" I said in a small voice.

"I want you to select a paddle, and after you do, I'm going to give you two swats."

These days, consumerism and choice are cornerstones of American culture. But this was my first experience at being offered a choice, other than the flavor of ice-cream I preferred. Frankly, none of these paddles looked all that appealing.

"I don't like any of them, sir."

"No, I expect not. But you need to choose, or I will choose for you."

I'd heard stories about these paddles. Only one kid, in the 10-year history of our school, had ever been paddled. We never knew what the crime was, or what happened to him after the highest form of punishment this side of the gas chamber.

We suspected he must have strangled the janitor or stolen a school bus.

Rumor had it that some of the paddles were lined with razor blades; others filled with lead.

As I retrieved these fragments from my fraying brain, Mr. Lewis tapped on his desk impatiently. I looked again, and it was like a game show where you had to decide which door held the least-unpleasant surprise. There was a very wide, short paddle, a long, rod-like paddle, and one somewhere in between that had holes in it like my mother's cheese grater.

"I'm afraid I can't wait any longer." Mr. Lewis reached towards them short paddle.

"No, the long one," I said, figuring I'd outsmart the principal by avoiding what was clearly his preferred instrument of pain.

"Very well. Now step over here," and he motioned a place on the floor just two steps from his chair. I stood there, and couldn't believe what was happening. I'd never been spanked in my life, and I was trying to figure out what made this time so different. I figured it must have been particularly terrible.

"I'm sorry."

"I'm sure you are. Bend over, please, and grasp your ankles."

"Can I explain?" I asked, stalling, hoping that the phone would ring, like in the movies when the convict is spared the electric chair and someone would run in and shout: "No! Stop! There's been a reprieve by the governor!"

But that didn't happen. Mr. Lewis did give me a moment to talk, and he asked me, as he had so many times before, "Why did you do that?"

My answer, as usual: "Uh… it seemed like a good idea at the time."

Unfortunately, that was not enough to save me.

"You need to bend over now. Unless you'd prefer three swats."

"No, sir."

So, I did as I was told, and looked out at the playground. It was filled with happy children. They whooped and played on the swings. They jumped rope. I, on the other hand, was bent over, butt upward.

I peeked behind me and saw Mr. Lewis, paddle in hand.

Mr. Lewis was not what you'd call a large man, perhaps he stood 5' 6," but at that moment, he looked like Godzilla in human form. He brought the paddle back to his shoulders, and let it fly.

The narrow rod, chosen by me in my inexperience in such matters, cut through my blue jeans and burned like I'd sat on my grandmother's heating vent. I had hardly begun to cry when the second blow hit me, this time lower and across my upper thighs, leaving me hurting in a whole new region.

"You are excused to wait outside," he said, and I left without turning to face him.

Tears were flowing as I walked out to stand by Mrs.

Earl. She glanced at me, and then mercifully looked back into the stack of papers on her desk. "Please sit down," she said. I did as I was told.

I learned that you are twice punished when you get swats: once in the getting and again in the sitting. I jumped up, the pain searing ever more intently. Mrs. Earl glared at me, and I slowly, painfully, sat back down.

I could not tell you, then or now, just what I said or did to get whacked. But I can tell you that on that day my approximate pulse rate was 190 beats a minute, because that's how many searing blasts of pain I got every minute during the next half-hour I waited until I was released.

Finally, it was 4 pm and I was free to go. Or, more correctly, I was free to walk out of the room.

My backside still sore, I ambled up the street with a John Wayne-like cadence. But, at long last I was home. Mom greeted me at the door, her fever having broken and Dad gone back to work.

"Have a nice day?" she asked innocently. She was just getting on her feet, and still too groggy to see my red face or awkward gait.

"Ah, I had ... to stay late," I said.

"I see." She yawned. "That's unfortunate. Can you get me a drink of water? I need to get back to bed. But I wanted to say hello." She gave me a hug, and it burned to lean into it, but I did.

She went back to her room, and I reflected on my day. I learned that the maximum punishment a school could dish out could strike at any odd time, for no apparent reason, and without prompting anyone at home to do anything other than ask for a glass of water.

It made no sense, and it didn't stop me from impulsively talking in class. Yet, I was never again paddled for that offense, which baffled me all the more.

It wasn't until *much* later that my mother learned of my paddling, and she contacted the school, unbeknownst to me, and told them it was *never* again to happen.

For years I held the dubious honor of being only one of two kids paddled in at Highland Elementary School. And, still, I had no clear memory of the offense that triggered this upgraded consequence.

Not long ago, curiosity got the better of me, and so I asked my dad, many years after my mother had died, just what I'd done.

"It must have been something particularly awful," I said, bracing myself for a horrible revelation.

"Oh, I don't remember." Dad scratched his head. Then he laughed. "Oh, yeah, that was the time your mom was sick and I answered the phone."

He then told me that, although he'd forgotten the offense, it was his idea to have me whacked. The paddling was a random act of paternal prerogative.

I was astonished, and asked him the obvious question: "Why?"

Dad shrugged and smiled a wicked grin.

"Hell," he said, "it seemed like a good idea at the time."

ACKNOWLEDGEMENTS

This collection of stories was written over several years with help from my writing group: Jim Dowling, Kathryn Gessner, Carla Jackson, Melinda Kashuba, and Charlie Price. Much of what is good in these stories is due to their sage advice.

Our group grew out of a writing class taught by Tony D'Souza, and we're all indebted to him.

My daughter Amanda has helped me with her keen proofreading and editing. And, of course, my wife and best friend Karin has been a constant source of encouragement and support. Thank you both for your help and for putting up with my quirky sense of humor.

Thanks, too, to my beta-readers: Susan Crandell, Barry Hilchey, Ken Lengel, and Venkat Raman. You've been most helpful in spotting glitches that got by me, despite several readings.

A very special thanks to the many teachers I've had along the way. Mister Paul was the first one who truly inspired me, but there have been many since then in various subject areas. I owe you more than words can say.

Finally, a few words of gratitude for my late mother,

Dr. Kodo Lightfoot. I owe the debt all children owe plus much, much more. Mom never made me feel like a bad person, just a bit misguided at times. But through it all I knew I was loved and appreciated. She could discipline me, and still laugh.

And that's the *best* medicine for any hyperactive kid.

Robb Lightfoot
Palo Cedro, California
December 2015

ABOUT THE AUTHOR

Robb Lightfoot lives with Karin, his wife of 33 years, in Northern California. His work has appeared in www.anewscafe.com and The Funny Times. He's been on stage as a warm-up act in Reno, and enjoys teaching communication and performance classes at Shasta Community College.

You can contact him at robb@thinkingfunny.com or PO Box 5286, Chico, CA, 95928.

Problem Child: The View From The Principal's Office is his fourth book.

PS—Front and rear cover photos are actual snapshots of me, circa 1958. I was three years old.

Made in the USA
Middletown, DE
01 December 2022

16694534R00099